Leela
Eny
is your life –
I love you bigger
than the Universe ?
Mom   6/30/21

Dancing with the Divine:
An earthly journey of
awakening

Katy

Dancing with the Divine: An earthy journey of awakening
By Katharine W. Locke

ISBN-13: 978-1-7358111-1-6

Mystery School Press
P.O. Box 63767
Philadelphia, PA 19147
mysteryschoolpress.com

Cover design by Silvia Rodriguez

Dancing with the Divine

An earthly journey of awakening

Katy Locke

MYSTERY SCHOOL PRESS

Philadelphia, Pennsylvania

Acknowledgements

I wish to thank many people without whom this work would not have seen the light of day: a revered college professor for her challenging questions about its first draft which left me puzzling and pondering for another twenty-five years; many tectonic teachers and mentors near and dear to my heart who changed my world again and again; my writing partner, for her enthusiasm and support through many months of uncertain unfolding; a dear friend for her eagle-eyed insightful feedback; my esteemed editor for her intrepid editorial comments worth their weight in gold, for her nitpicky attention to detail, fearless questions, helpful suggestions, and especially for her hilarious illuminations of the glaringly obvious! And finally, my publisher, for his spiritual clarity and guidance, and his commitment to support emerging "Artists of Possibility" in our own becoming.

"There has, in my view, been a tendency to discount and marginalize the importance of our embodied nature, as though it were something incidental about us, rather than essential to us...."

—Iain McGilChrist,
The Master and his Emissary:
the Divided Brain and the Making of the Western World

Contents

The Key

*"Truly, it is in the darkness that one finds the light,
so when we are in sorrow, then this light is nearest
of all to us."*

—Meister Eckhart

FALL, 1964

I'LL NEVER FORGET THE clutch in my stomach, the
trembling in my five-year-old arms and legs, and my wildly
beating and breaking heart as I marched out through the
living room double doors onto the chill, unforgiving stone
porch, and down onto the asphalt driveway, to stare blank-
ly at the long, indistinct pile of oak leaves, my mother's
angry voice resounding loudly in my head.

Whatever had possessed me, a few days earlier, in the
presence of my elder sister, to close the dark oak door of
the third floor storage closet, to grasp, cool and smooth
between my thumb and forefinger, the ringed end of the

skeleton key protruding from the classically crafted key-hole, and turn it until it clicked with a satisfying tumble of the lock? Whatever had possessed me to pocket the key, and wander downstairs to the first floor and out onto the driveway where my father was raking leaves? And whatever had drawn my attention away from the leaves, to unknown imaginary adventures, so that I removed the key from my pocket and placed it (or hid it?) quite deliberately under a particular pile of oak leaves now raked to one side of the driveway in temporary station before their final haul down to the curb?

And what had possessed me to forget all about it until a week later when a stern summons from my mother brought me into her bedroom face-to-face with her beet red and fuming visage, as she demanded that I return the key immediately *or else!* while my sister stood by looking down at her feet?

It was the unspecified nature of the *or else!* that unleashed the darkest recesses of my imagination, and overwhelmed the delicate extremes of my sensitive nervous system in this moment out on the driveway, filling me with the most abject yet familiar self-loathing and self-hatred.

Why am I so bad?! How could I have done this stupid, stupid thing?!

As my sister stood allied with my mother's righteous cause, I was cast out, abandoned and alone in my guilt, shame, and peril, with the certainty that there was no hope for me—all was lost.

As I gazed at the now matted leaves much altered by a week of rain, I had no idea—not a shred of hope—whether this was in fact where I had de-pocketed and deposited the key. Were these the same leaves, miraculously undisturbed, or not?

A primal wail arose in my throat as my body expelled a tantrum of stomping feet and flailing arms. I wished I had never been born! That my poor, wretched life had never come to this!

Spent, hoarse, dry-eyed, I took three steps to the spot I vaguely remembered I might have chosen at the crest of the driveway between its long level advance to the garage and its steep descent to the street, squatted down, and with agonized longing in my heart extended two hands to scoop up a double-clutch of wet leaves.

At the same time that I didn't believe it would actually be there, nor that I deserved even to have it be so, nor truly deserved any outcome other than the very worst, I did at that moment close my eyes and say a brief prayer for my own salvation, *Please, God, please!* and in so doing set a slightly altered course for my confusing and tortured life that in this moment now included a tiny but unquenchable glimmer of hope.

And there, before my eyes when I dared open them, damp but distinct amidst earthy decomposition, was the key.

INTRODUCTION:
The Intention

"But while others did not seem out of place in the bleak modern landscape, some remnant of Eden remained in her soul and made her an outsider."

—Gary Lachman, *The Lost knowledge of the Imagination*

THE JOURNEY YOU ARE about to embark upon in reading this book relates the tale of my "earthly journey of awakening." What, pray, is that?! Good question.

What I cannot begin to answer here are the deeper why's of the human experience: Why do we apparently agree to forget the divinity of who we truly are when we enter this world, and then spend our lives trying to remember it? Why are some lives seemingly so cursed and others so blessed? Why, if we are all equally loved by the Divine, do some of us insist on perpetrating horrors upon ourselves and each other? I don't know. What I do answer in this book is the question of how, in the midst of my own thickly opaque human experience, divine insight, love, and guidance did appear, did leave clues, and did gently guide me to awaken.

While I was raised with a Protestant identity, my family was not active within any specific church or religious tradition. For eleven formative years, I was enrolled in a Quaker school, and attended the required weekly Quaker Meeting for ten of them—for which we were gently instructed that the divine light exists within all of us, and so we gather in silence to listen for the voice of God. I remember one trimester of Quakerism in seventh grade in which the Bible was mentioned—though not studied. Otherwise, Quaker values of equality, simplicity, and pacifism were woven into the fabric of my primary and secondary education, leaving me with no particular religious convictions or any sense of what divinity might be.

The direction I anticipated my life would take was: college, perhaps graduate school, career, love, career, marriage, career, family, career, retirement. Instead, the direction my life took was: college, medical-leave, psychotherapeutic intervention, gourmet cafeteria omelette-maker, square dancing, first love, college-attempt #2, college withdrawal #2, apprentice stringed-musical-instrument repair, homesteading, waitressing, apprentice patternmaking for a cast iron wood stove company, ongoing homesteading, apprentice architecturally designed high-end corporate office furniture making ... you get the idea. My life did not unfold according to any plan I ever made, or anyone ever made for me. It just happened, full of many twists and turns I eventually came to call "labyrinthine." And it is only now, looking back, that I am able to assemble this journey into what I hope is a coherent and accessible narrative.

At the age of 21, after a two-year medical leave from college, I transferred to a university closer to home where something happened to dramatically change my life. I enrolled in a course called Folklore and the Supernatural, thinking I would like to learn more about folklore because during my leave of absence I had become active in the local folk community. As it turned out, the class was not about folklore so much as it was about the supernatural, and it exposed me to a whole host of new perspectives on the nature of reality. I read about unexplained synchronicities in nature, paranormal phenomena, psychic and spiritual healers, including a persecuted one in Brazil who would cure people of all kinds of dire ailments by sticking a rusty knife into their eye sockets while he himself was possessed with various healing spirits guiding his actions. Horrifying, but apparently true!

Fresh from these exciting and unexpected reading assignments, I would walk into class and gaze adoringly at my professor. Afterwards, I would walk out feeling like my head was going to explode. This seeded a desire to develop my own supernatural, or extraordinary, capabilities, though I had no idea what they might be or how to go about it. I only knew that they could be described as non-rational or non-intellectual and so I decided to drop out of college, this time for good, setting the rather vague intention that I would allow more space in my brain for other things to occur. When I proudly presented this momentous decision to my much admired professor he was aghast that I would give up the privilege of a college education. I, on the other hand, was aghast that he was not both flattered and pleased that his class had impacted me on such a deep level. I left the meeting embarrassed and disappointed, but resolute.

During the next several years, this rather abstract intention was lost to my conscious mind, buried under the demands of the working-girl life to which I now subscribed. For about a decade, I worked anywhere from sixty to eighty hours a week as a waitress and woodworker, in addition to many dutiful hours as a wife and homesteader. Rarely a day off, let alone a vacation, so focused was I on building a down-home, country dream with my boyfriend-turned-husband. Nevertheless, in the midst of this whirlwind life, strange encounters with the natural world started inserting themselves into moments when I wasn't looking. They were so outside of any recognizable reality that at the same time I held them as secret and precious, I also promptly forgot about them.

As fate would have it, the down-home, country dream turned nightmare and by my mid-thirties, the marriage, waitressing, woodworking, and homesteading had been abandoned, and a college degree procured after all. But at that time, finding myself alone and debilitated by a mysterious set of symptoms known as "chronic fatigue," memories of these mysterious events started coming back to me. Each day, with what little energy I could muster, I typed them up and was soon forced to acknowledge that they were both numerous and extraordinary. I hoped someday I would share them, perhaps in a book.

That book has taken another twenty-five years to crystalize. And what I have only just come to appreciate is that, in its own inexplicable way, the intention I set at university has mysteriously come to pass. Even though I kept trying to take my daily life in other directions, it kept coming back to the extraordinary, the miraculous, the mystical, and the paranormal. And only slowly have I come to understand that from the moment I prayed for that lost storage closet key, I have been seeking a more perfect union with the Divine—and for whatever reason that union has been most accessible to me in nature. My life has been a quest to understand and articulate what it means to be a spiritual being having a human experience, dancing uncertainly at the intersection between matter and ether; between hope, possibility, perfection, and inspiration on the one hand, and despair, impenetrability, disaster, and feet of clay on the other.

Around the age of forty, still in the thick of the confusion and under-accomplishment that seemed to describe my life, I had a first astrological reading of my natal chart which revealed some major themes. As we reviewed the unique attributes and challenges that defined my growth and development in this lifetime, I learned that the main signifier in my chart was creativity in the midst of the element of earth on the one hand, and fire on the other. "Earth and fire don't naturally understand one another," I was told. And yet, here I was in this lifetime, trying to embody these opposing qualities, energies, and properties through a journey of creativity. This, then, was the reason for my incarnation.

For many years I have pondered what it might mean to me that earth and fire don't naturally understand one another. To me, the element of earth is grounded, dense, solid, staid, obstinate, embodied, sensual, practical, plodding, hands-on, lending itself to the concrete daily tasks of living. Fire on the other hand is HOT! Gaseous, dangerous, burning, consuming, life-threatening, expressive, ebullient, brilliant, inspirational, spiritual, heavenly, essential, sparking, life-giving, life-taking. Combine fire and water, and you get steam. Combine fire and air and you get more fire. But combine fire and earth and you get: magma—deep thick oceans of untouchable molten material; or smothering and smoking; or fired clay pottery; or malleable iron or liquid steel, copper, or gold.

Furnaces are not places we can inhabit, but we benefit from the outcomes, from their alchemical transformations. Bedrock was once in a furnace. Now it is not. It is the absence of fire that allows us to stand upon the Earth and make our lives here, yet we could not live without the distant sun. On the other hand, we can't fly too high or our waxen wings will melt and we will plummet back to Earth. There is tension here. In my case, I believe it is this tension that forged my spirituality, that freed my spirit to be able to express itself in nature, and through nature; to swell with the very essence of the spirit of life emanating from every tree, every rock, every leaf and flower, every mountain and hill, river and stream. I was gradually hammering out something entirely new to my consciousness. I was not brought up to worship in the woods—to worship at all. I did not find my god in heaven; instead, my divinity, or goddess, expressed herself from the Earth.

This creative tension has shown up in countless ways that have both bedeviled and bemused me. In dismay at living such a tumultuous life for so many years, I have been unconsciously thinking that my ultimate goal was to bring order, control, to make sense of it all. But as you will see, this book is a testament to the impossibility of such an aspiration. I am surrendering instead to the fact that being human is just plain messy. A spiritual being having a human experience is, by design, embodying two elements—earth (flesh, matter) and fire (spirit, divinity)—that don't naturally understand one another.

Even though these two elements of earth and fire so often operate at cross-purposes in my life, the resulting alchemy has yielded something unique and valuable after all—a fully embodied divinity dancing upon the Earth. Should your earthly journey be similarly full of twists and turns that don't naturally understand one another, it is my hope that in my story you will find, arising from the sticky molasses of human imperfection, new possibilities in the unfolding freedom, clarity, serenity, and ecstasy in dancing with the Divine, or rather having the Divine dancing with you.

Early Imprints

1959–1985

"Perhaps, even more than the surfeit of touch that so many human beings experience, it is the lack of Earth and plant song that causes so much alienation and emptiness."

—Stephen Harrod Buhner, *Sacred Plant Medicine*

CHAPTER ONE

Certain Imperfections

"Illness performs a crucial and important function: it allows the de-structuring of a contemporary state, readying the organism for change."

—Stephen Harrod Buhner, *Sacred Plant Medicine*

WHEN I TURNED FOUR, my relatively stable family life turned upside down. In very short order, my maternal grandfather, on the verge of retirement, died of a stroke, my father lost his job, my mother lost a pregnancy, and our family of six left its home. For the previous four years, my parents had been living their dream in Colorado, having moved from New England only a few months after I was born. My father's dismissal was under mysterious circumstances, but he quickly found a new job as vice-principal of a boarding school in the sleepy rural town of Steamboat Springs where the family moved into faculty housing.

My memories of that year are sparse, but distinct: of being the only sibling not yet in school, of being at home with my mother, who was always in her Chinese-red bathrobe (my mother would later say she was very depressed and drinking a lot); of playing alone by the side of a stream that ran by our house and losing my plastic watering can into the spring surge, and desperately wanting to go in after it but hesitating on the bank; of walking alone and terrified a long way down our dirt road one day (half a mile, my mother would later estimate) to my friend's house, only to have him not want to play with me.

Years later my mother would tell me that when my grandmother encountered me the summer after that year, she announced with great import, "Katy's changed." I don't know exactly who I had been before that, but I remember distinctly who I had become: a chubby tomboy, obsessed with wanting to be a boy and suffering the cruel daily realities of being "just a girl," with very low self-esteem and adept at entertaining herself. We had just moved back east to Pennsylvania for my father's new job as head of a private elementary school. At my father's urging, my mother reluctantly returned to the demands of full-time classroom teaching to fill a vacancy. On the verge of entering kindergarten, and already having learned not to make demands of her, I didn't even question how thoroughly my young needs got lost in this new shuffle.

While fragile and confused on the inside, I was full of bravado and rambunctious creativity on the outside, known for making grand pronouncements for which I had no real knowledge or backing. Imaginary games with friends were my idea of heaven, and I would play them for as many hours as I was allowed, always pretending to be a boy. My relationship with my body in those days was fraught: I hated being a girl, hated the way I looked and hated the way I felt, and most of all hated my powerlessness in a boy-focused world where all the good characters in books and all the good characters on TV (at least the ones I knew of) were boys. There was Little League baseball for my brother but not for me. Men/boys, it seemed, had all the power and attention, and that made me mad.

Challenges with food came honestly: my mother modeled her own dysfunction through endless declarations of body-image self loathing, bingeing, and chronic crash dieting. When I was six, she insisted that I hold my stomach in. I stared at thin bodies everywhere—at school, at the pool or the beach—and I so longed to be in one of them. When I was nine, my mother asked me if I wanted to take on a dieting challenge where for one year I would have no second helpings, and eat only fruit between meals. The reward? Ten dollars, an unimaginable fortune! Of course I wanted to please her, and of course I had no sense of what this would entail, so I said, "Yes!" My resolve lasted about a day, and for another 364 I sneaked and cheated and wallowed in guilt and fear of discovery. When my annual date rolled around, I signed up for another year, thinking I could make up for the first one, but alas I failed again. More guilt, more shame, more fear. And all the more reason to maintain a safe distance from her so I wouldn't get found out.

Not infrequently, I was home sick and miserable with throat infections, mumps, bronchitis, etc., staring out my bedroom window as siblings and neighbors played outside. As often as I could get away with, I also made up symptoms so I could stay home from school and watch TV. I suffered painful digestive issues that would go undiagnosed well into middle age, and the combination of too many antibiotics administered to an already sensitive and compromised physiological system no doubt contributed to a series of both chronic and acute health challenges throughout my adult years.

And so my childhood was full of secrets: secret longings, secret feelings, secret obsessions; I lied and stole, and rarely got caught. I didn't justify it, I just couldn't help myself. I had lots of friends, and could afford to be mean sometimes, which I was. It wasn't until age fourteen that I played my last imaginary game as a boy. I made myself stop by sheer force of will because I could no longer pretend that my body wasn't developing into that of a young woman. I unwittingly turned my obsessive tendencies toward eating disorders: a couple of years of near anorexia, followed by several more years of junk-food bingeing and dramatic weight gain.

During this time, I dreamed of becoming the next Olga Korbut, Nadia Comaneci, or Judith Jameson: to have a thin, muscular, long-legged body that flew effortlessly through space and time—instead of my long torso, wide hips, and short legs, not to mention generous and unruly breasts which required nothing less than the proverbial "over-the-shoulder-boulder-holder" to keep them reasonably well contained. Despite enrolling in both gymnastics and dance lessons, I just couldn't seem to rise above eating addictions, body obsessions, anxiety, marginal health, physical pain, or emotional distress. It was hard enough just to get through each day.

By age sixteen, my body was round, voluptuous—and numb. Intermittent panic attacks erupted in waves of tremors and contractions in my arms and legs. On the first occasion, my parents took me to the emergency room, but the doctor just sent us home without any recommendations. So while developing prize-winning academic capacities, I was increasingly left behind socially and emotionally. Compared to the inclinations of my friends toward parties, dating, testing boundaries, and sex, all I wanted to do after school was binge on candy bars and donuts.

This well-hidden sugar addiction helped me make it through high school looking like a success but feeling like a failure. I earned straight A's, won academic awards, sang solos, danced, and performed on stage. I told everyone my college choice was because of its performing arts program, but actually it was because my mother went there. I had heard her tell stories of having had mischievous fun in college, and so I thought I would, too. Instead, I became very depressed and took a medical leave halfway through my sophomore year. I went home and entered psychotherapy, initially four days a week. For a few months, therapy was the only focus in my life. I lived at home, watched TV, ate whatever, and dragged myself to session after session for one hour each day.

For the first time, I stopped merely getting by and brought my attention to a very confusing inner life. I had to learn to talk about lots of things to which I had never given voice. It was both reassuring and terrifying. And the things that would not come out of my mouth during appointments, found their way onto paper in between. While lying on the sofa in my therapist's dimly lit office, I discovered that when my words ran out, I could stare at the ceiling and make the whole room disappear. My therapist would say, "Katy, where have you gone?" to which I would reply, "I don't know." Many years later I would understand this as a kind of dissociation. But in the moment, it was simply a relief to be able to dissolve into nothingness.

One day, in the midst of a conversation about a new romantic interest, a guy I had met at a barn dance, my therapist said to me, "Well, I don't know if there really is any such thing as true happiness in life." To this day, I don't exactly know why she inserted that into our conversation in exactly that way, but at the time I was heartbroken for her because somehow inside of my upside-down and inside-out life I was absolutely sure there was such thing as true happiness even though I didn't know if I would ever find it, or even recognize it if I did. Over the next eleven years, as the new romance progressed into a rocky marriage and ended in divorce, I would have to admit that I hadn't even remotely begun to find the happiness I sought, though I still believed it possible.

CHAPTER TWO

Earth, Air, Fire, & Water

"The Earth is a large hologram of spirit: in each of its parts the whole of spirit exists and can be experienced. Our connection to spirit then begins with our connection to the Earth and the elements that sustain life."

—Pam Montgomery, *Plant Spirit Healing*

BOTH MY PARENTS SHARED a deep appreciation for the outdoors. While the heart-wrenching complexities of human intercourse so often confused, overwhelmed, and befuddled, the simple, sensual, and awe-inspiring gifts of the natural world enveloped, embraced, and comforted. My parents met as elementary school interns at a private school in Massachusetts and married a year after they graduated. With elementary education as the family business, my siblings and I enjoyed generous vacations which afforded much room for open-ended adventures in fields, woods, mountains, wind, storms, rain, sun, ocean, and lakes. And these elemental building blocks of life would one day come to characterize my first conscious explorations into the Divine.

In contrast to the demands of the school year and the physical isolation of our large, rambling, and often not-very-well-kept stone house, summer, winter, and spring vacations offered spacious family time inhabiting close and simple quarters at a cottage by the sea, or cabins by a lake, and later, a farmhouse in Vermont. My parents modeled a poetic delight in the sights, sounds, and smells of these moments: listening for gulls, osprey, or owls; melding with the roar of surf or rhythmic pounding of lake water on shore; tasting fresh salty breezes or scoping skies for new cloud formations, wind or weather indicating approaching storms; glorying in the varied palettes of lingering summer sunsets.

These imprints inspired me to various childhood outdoor endeavors: running barefoot over piercing pebbles on our dirt road; enduring the simultaneous prickle and tickle of salt marsh grasses on bare soles and ankles; braving the primal unknowns of dark estuarine ooze between my toes; curling my toes to clutch at soft tickling sands sucked out from underfoot by overlapping waves at the ocean's edge; learning to sail from my elder brother whose extreme tactics scared me to death; galloping double-bareback through fields or on riding trails and over natural jumps; sneaking on to the public beach at night with my elder siblings and their teenage friends to skinny dip.

On the Massachusetts coast, we spent days on end at the beach, swimming in the waves, riding the surf, building sand-castles, exploring extensive dunes; picnicking aboard our first tiny, then increasingly larger, sailboats, absorbing the delicate and delicious dance of navigating wind, tide, shoals, and sun. Without the distracting addiction of TV more typical of the school year, summer evenings were spent walking on the beach, playing cards, gathering with local kids for kick-the-can or capture-the-flag, reading aloud, and a weekly Saturday night square dance. Once, when I was six or seven, my father told me that there was to be a moonlight sail after the dance that night. And sure enough, around 10:00 p.m., we walked down the lane to the now shadowy little beach where our ten-foot day-sailer was moored, and were soon under way.

Under clear skies and a full moon, with an extra high moon tide flooding the tidal river, a small flotilla of modest day-sailers skimmed noiselessly over the water like ghosts. Propelled by a gentle breeze, we made our way effortlessly around and over the tips of salt marsh grasses, the only visible indication of the dark chunky mudflats submerged below, and weaved our way on either side of the main channel between stationary larger craft straining against their mooring lines. Without the usual buzz of motor boats large and small, fishing boats, cars, or lawnmowers, the quiet was startling.

Leaning my chin on my hands gripping the gunnel of our O'Day Sprite, I let my eyes be dazzled by the brilliant moonlight above in her watery reflections below. I was astonished at how our journey was at the same time so full of darkness and yet so full of light. As my gaze travelled further outwards, it was filled with surreal images of gliding white triangular and quadrilateral sails set in stark contrast against the deep, dark abyss of distant water which itself blended seamlessly into blackened trees along the shore. In that ethereal silence was perhaps my first sweet kiss of the Divine.

On intermittent summers, my family made a long trek to northern Ontario to my mother's family island camp on a pristine and wild lake. At a young age, I was inducted into her family tradition of starting each day with a chilly skinny dip off the main dock, after which I remember donning layers of warm clothing and hurrying up to the main cabin for hot Red River cereal, bacon, eggs, and crispy toast baked in a wood-fired oven. Throughout long luscious days, on many trips back and forth between the dock, the water's edge, the outhouse, the sleeping cabins and the main cabin, I bonded readily to the pungent smell of the red pine needles and cones, and the feel of irregular roots underfoot.

In the evenings after dinner dishes were done, there were often lazy canoe rides around the large island. Sometimes I would paddle the bow, sometimes ride on a cushion in the middle of the canoe with my parents at bow and stern, immersed in the magic of this gentle time of day. Amidst the rhythmic strokes of paddles, we pointed to an early evening star, or an occasional leap of fish, lulled by the deeply primal cascading calls of loons up and down the lake, some nearby and some echoing from miles away. Afterwards, back in the main cabin, we shared reading aloud and card games under the quiet roar and faltering glow of Coleman lantern light. And perhaps once a summer, we might attend a square dance at the family camp across the lake.

From age eight, I was groomed to be a strong and able paddler, in calm waters and rough, in sun, rain, and wind. I learned to hold my own in the bow of our classic chestnut and canvas canoes, sometimes empty and tippy, other times heavily laden with gear destined for daylong picnics or overnight camping. Unbelievably, we drank water directly from the lake. Campsites in the many breathtaking arms and inlets were there for the picking. Once established, we pitched tents, unrolled sleeping bags, endured mosquitos, and rejuvenated with campfire cooking, hot cocoa, s'mores, and the mesmerizing glow of dying embers. Eventually we would trundle off to bed with smoky clothing and hair, falling into a deep and satisfying, if somewhat root-ridden, slumber.

When I was eleven, my parents bought a farmhouse in Vermont, and thus commenced our family tradition of spending Thanksgiving, Christmas to New Year, and spring vacations at the farm. We enjoyed downhill skiing at various mountains, and cross-country skiing and skating in the countryside closer to home. We took long walks through fields and woods up the back hill behind the house. And at all times of day or night we went sledding, tobogganing, as well as whizzing uncontrollably down that same steep hill on thick sheets of plastic we had found in the barn. In the summers, we hiked four-thousand-footers with our cousins in sun, fog, and rain; went canoeing and swimming; and, for me, horseback riding at overnight camp.

Retreating to Vermont during the school year framed these holidays in a warm glow, much like the radiant heat of the wood stoves at either end of the house. Whereas back in Philly I resented having an uncomfortably chilly bedroom, at the farmhouse I braced myself heartily to slide between cold sheets, and marveled at the frost buildup on the *inside* of my window panes. Cutting our own Christmas trees on the back hill, as lopsided and imperfect as they inevitably were, settled a down-home charm in my heart.

CHAPTER THREE

Strange Stirrings

"Our life is a faint tracing on the surface of mystery…"

—Annie Dillard, *Pilgrim at Tinker Creek*

FROM FIRST THROUGH FIFTH grade, my best friend lived next door. And although we didn't go to the same school during the day, we spent as much time together as we could after school and on weekends. Our favorite activities were imaginary games, sometimes fashioned after TV shows or books, and sometimes just arising out of the fertile void of our collaborative imaginations: Batman and Robin, Maya (the elephant), Super Boy and Super Girl, Twins, and the list goes on. The one most vivid for me was Tarzan and Jai, with jungles, swinging vines, raging rivers, chimpanzees, and all manner of other wild beasts. Endless after-school and weekend hours over those five formative years stretched to near eternity.

The summer before sixth grade, my best friend's family moved away and a new family with five children moved in for one year with a boy nearly my age. He and I hit it off, playing imaginary games of our own (army, mostly), splashing around in our above-ground pool, and going to the movies. One notable evening, we sat in his front yard and talked about reincarnation, trying to work out the mysteries of our existence. We both agreed that while having a series of lives seemed compelling, we couldn't quite wrap our minds around going on forever. Better than up and just ending, though. One of our favorite activities was to go running in the rain. Spring would bring torrential cloud bursts, sometimes but not always accompanied by lightning and thunder. Drenching ourselves in downpours exhilarated beyond belief. We would run, and splash and laugh rebelliously, not caring that we would return with our uncomfortably sodden clothes sticking to our skin, and our shoes leaden and squelchy.

One spring afternoon years later, after the boy had moved away, I was out in the back yard with my elder sister. I don't remember what we were doing out there, but it was during a time when we were not particularly close, certainly not playful. She was turning her attention to graduating from high school and going away to college and I was struggling with depression and weight gain in the midst of also receiving the romantic attention of an older boy at school. Anyway, suddenly it threatened to rain, and our first instinct was to gather our things to go inside. But without prior thought, I found myself suddenly wanting to stay out and be in the rain, and tried to convince my sister to stay with me. When she declined, I grabbed her hands and pulled on her to stay, during which a downpour began in earnest. After a few moments of the drenching deluge, she gave in and we returned to the back yard to dance and prance around, singing and laughing together. Afterwards, I thanked her for staying out with me, and she admitted, "That was fun!" I felt curiously validated that she would actually enjoy something so spontaneous and wacky, instigated by her younger sister.

Two random occurrences in spring of my freshman year at college would eventually prove significant, although it would be many years later that I even remembered them. The first followed a viewing of "Brother Sun, Sister Moon," a 1960s romanticized version of the awakening of St. Francis of Assisi that moved me to tears. I had never heard of St. Francis, or if I had, I never knew anything about him. I learned that he was an Italian 13th century monk known for his commitment to live in poverty and serve the poor, his love of wild animals, and that to him nature was a reflection of God. Sometime in the next several weeks, I found myself taking a shortcut through some woods on campus that I had never noticed before. I'm not even sure there was a path, although I imagine there was. In any case, I found myself progressing a bit cluelessly until much to my surprise I came across a larger than life-sized statue of a monk with outstretched arms and hands adorned with wild animals. Sure enough, the inscription identified him as St. Francis. Stunned and moved, I stopped and spent an awkward moment with him, feeling a strange stir of kinship. Then, I continued on to my next class.

The other happened the following spring when I was walking under a large, still-leafless oak tree outside of my dorm.

I had a strange and uninvited thought: *I wonder how I look to this tree? It's so big, and its lifeline is so long by comparison that I must look rather ant-like, my movements jerky and speeded up, sort of like an ant looks to me.* Although it had no precedent or context, the thought even then struck me as notably curious. *Where did that come from?* And even though I forgot about it at the time, it would come back to me years later when I was remembering other such inexplicable moments in nature.

CHAPTER FOUR

Life on "The Branch"

*"The secret of seeing is to sail on solar wind. Hone
and spread your spirit till you yourself are a sail,
whetted, translucent, broadside to the merest puff."*

—Annie Dillard, *Pilgrim at Tinker Creek*

FALL, 1983

MY SOON-TO-BE-HUSBAND AND I moved from
Pennsylvania to Vermont with almost no money, no defi-
nite employment, but with a truckload of woodworking
tools and all our dreams. We had arranged to rent my parents' farmhouse, remotely located in a dairy farming valley.
I found work immediately, first a daytime job at a college
cafeteria, and then waitressing on nights and weekends.
For the next seven years or so, working from morning 'til
night seven days a week was almost all I did—and when
not at work I was busy doing household chores including
growing, cooking, and freezing organic vegetables to support our vegetarian lifestyle.

My memories of that first winter were: unending snow, from November to April; cold, where the only relief was to hold hands and feet right up against a roaring wood stove; and darkness. A long awaited spring was heralded first by winds. They whipped down the valley from the north as if to rattle and shake the trees out of their stupor. I wondered if the trees pruned their dead wood that way to prepare for the new growing season. But no matter how welcoming the reluctantly warming weather seemed, the trees simply refused to leaf out. My husband and I watched and waited upon them through April and we watched and waited upon them through May, flabbergasted that they did not leaf out until June first. Thinking back, we realized that almost all the leaves had fallen by October first the previous fall. Compared to Pennsylvania, where trees had leaves from April through November, that was eight long, cold months without leaves. Only four months with leaves? *What were we thinking?*

Imagine my delight, then, at the first real cloudburst with thunder, lightning, and a clean wash of torrential rain. I went out on the porch and gazed at the flowering apple tree across the road. Despite the ongoing chill in the air, I really wanted to run in this rain, to be in this rain, to lose myself in this rain.

"I want to take my clothes off and go run in the rain," I said.

"Go ahead," said my husband.

"Really?" I responded, surprised. "But what if someone drives by and sees me?"

"No one's going to see you," he assured me. "Besides, if they come up the road then just run back in the house."

"I dunno." I debated with myself. "Oh, okay!" What the hell, right? The struggle was less about what was outside of me and more about what was inside of me: shame, embarrassment, mixed with all the pent-up exhilaration of surviving the dark, cold demands of our first full winter.

I untied my boots and pulled them off as quickly as I could, hopping around on the opposite foot with each one. I unbuttoned my flannel shirt and off it came, along with corduroy pants, wool socks, waffle-style long underwear, everything off. Hunching protectively with my arms crossed over my breasts, I stepped out on to the porch. The warm spring air teased me forward while streaks of chilled air rose up from the still thawing ground. But the tree, and the rain, all that glorious rain ... I screamed and went for it. I ran out to the tree, screeching, shaking my hands, prancing my feet on the cold ground. My pendulous breasts flapped and flopped.

I immediately turned around and ran back to the porch, panting and laughing. Oh, it was not enough. Not enough! I looked all around, scouting for onlookers, until I was reasonably sure there were none. I ran out again, and this time I stayed by the tree, dancing around foolishly, but happily. I turned my face upwards to receive the full force of the rain. God, it was wonderful. What was it about rain? Even this chilly version of torrential spring rain, unleashing everything I'd bound up inside for so long? *Thank you. Thank you for this rain!*

A year later toward the end of April, I had a day off on the first unbelievably warm, sunny, picture-perfect spring day. Blue sky, not a cloud in sight. Snow only here and there where the plow had piled it up. Pungent smells arising from thawing ground. And somehow, miraculously, I wasn't working. I was here, at home, and could enjoy this day. I wanted to go for a walk up the back hill, but as I headed down the road, instead of following it across and up the other side, I cut off into the hayfield on my left and followed "The Branch," the colloquial name for a branch of a major local river, downstream. Its banks were still swollen with spring runoff. The stream-bed was fairly straight along that stretch, but the water twisted and twirled with lighthearted gurgles around leaning scrub trees and eroding dark chunks of rich, floodplain sod.

Spring in Vermont was still a mystery to me. The first year my husband and I had decided it was non-existent, that in fact it went directly from winter to summer, separated only by a little two-week comma, perhaps, called "Mud Season." This year, he had suggested that spring did exist but that it was subtle. Since the trees didn't leaf out until practically summer, basically, then spring was the time of buds.

"See?" he said to me one day while driving down the valley, pointing up into the ridges on either side. "See how the crowns of the trees are just beginning to change?" I looked.

At first, all I saw was the same old bleak, grey-brown hill I'd been staring at for six months.

"Change—?"

"Yeah. Just hints of colors, reddish, orange, green—"

"Oh, yeah!" I saw it. He was right. There it was. The hills were scalloped with muted colors. Changing. S L O W L Y. So then we tried subtle on for size to see if it didn't foster any greater sense of appreciation, aesthetic appeal, and patience.

The real mystery was, how could it be so hot and so cold all at once? The sun was HOT: on my head and on my exposed arms and legs. The air was cool. The ground was cold. And there was still snow, for heaven's sake! Basking in the warm rays as I walked along, I reached the swimming hole, where the water was four feet deep, and where growing up, we had found it wide enough for shallow dives off the bank.

The water was crystal clear. I could see all the way to the bottom. And gosh darn it if that speckled sunlight wasn't just dancing off the surface of The Branch, looking so *purty and invitin'* …. Inviting? No way! That water must be absolutely frigid! But the sun rays were still saying, "C'mon, it's so hot, how can you resist a little dip?" *Ay yi yi*. And, do you know what? Those goddamn rays were right. I couldn't resist. I couldn't resist! But I could go get a towel.

I ran back to the house. "I'm going for a swim!" I yelled to my husband.

"You crazy?" He asked with a half-smile and look of utter and total disbelief, regarding me with his knuckles on his hips, tipping a little forward on the balls of his feet.

"Totally." I smiled. I didn't know what else to say. I went into the bathroom and grabbed a towel, and off I went. Fortunately the sun was still hot. I was eager with anticipation and doubt, in a stalemate between the two. Standing again at the water's edge, it was again inviting me to come in. I sat down on the muddy embankment and dipped my toes in. Shit!!! It was cold. I slid down onto a small muddy ledge, and let my feet sink in. As I stood in the freezing, shin-deep water I knew that, even though I couldn't believe it, somehow I was going in. I had to.

I climbed back up on the bank and reached cross-armed for the tails of my shirt. I stopped and looked all around me for a long time. Then with firm resolve and exhilaration I yanked the shirt up and over my head. Everything came off. Soon, I was quivering on the bank of The Branch once again. I looked, I stared, I rocked, I breathed, I stared some more, I rocked, I yelled, I went. A full-fledged dive right in! I came up gasping, trying to catch my breath. I spun and reached for shore. *Ugh, nothing but a muddy bank.* But no matter, it was my only ticket out of there. I literally dragged myself up the bank, so thankful to be alive. And sooooo ALIVE! I looked down the front of me at the smear of mud and grass. It was awful and wonderful at the same time. Why is life so often like that? *Well, look at me!* I had to go in again and wash this stuff off. I was still psyched for it and dreading it, only more so. I did my little dance, rocking, swinging my arms, breathing, staring, only for not as long (or was it longer? I couldn't tell). I was in! I could breathe this time so I took a minute to swim. A short, wild, wonderful minute.

What was it about immersing myself naked in water? Why was I so drawn to it? Yes, in the moment it was exotically sensual to feel the water's caress down my front, down my back, and between my legs, with my normally heavy breasts bobbing lightheartedly at the surface. But looking back, I have to wonder if it was something deeper and more mysterious ... a purification of some kind? Was I trying to cleanse my body of painful imprints? Dissolve ancient patterns of self-loathing in my psyche? Wash away invisible stains of misogyny upon my soul? Or was it simply that breaking through inner barriers of fear and shame was unspeakably liberating, a clarion call to freedom? The combination of explosive movement and frigid temperatures released something ecstatic and ineffable, if only for a moment. Of course, none of this was conscious at the time. On the surface, I was just plain called to do these things. And I couldn't refuse.

I was out. That time, I stood up and climbed the bank like a respectably sane individual. There was mud only on my feet and calves. I toweled dry and dressed. *WOW. Swimming before the end of April. What a feat!* That would give me something to brag about for a while.

Awakenings

"On occasion, there may take place a sudden convergence of ... synchronicities, intricately interconnected, occurring in close proximity or in rapid succession, and having the effect of an overpowering epiphany of new meaning and purpose in the life of the individual."

—Richard Tarnas, *Cosmos and Psyche*

CHAPTER FIVE

A Winter's Walk

*"Our mystical journeys beyond our current dimen-
sionality are often impossible to communicate to
anyone else."*

—Jeff Carreira, *The Soul of a New Self*

SOLSTICE, 1985

THE UPSIDE OF THOSE years of working so intensely
was that I was acquiring many basic life skills: waitressing
was reasonably lucrative, and very transferrable; organic
gardening was putting food on the table or in the freezer;
my vegetarian cooking was becoming more adventurous
and tasty and I was amassing a stack of 3x5 cards with creative and original recipes. Among them was a vegetarian
holiday Solstice dinner that included homemade stuff-
ing with apples and chestnuts; mashed potatoes, butternut squash, and apple and pumpkin pie with whole wheat
crust and sweetened only with apple juice concentrate.

On one holiday, a rare day off, I had spent the morning
preparing such a feast. Tired of looking at food, I decided

to go for a walk. Although our intention in moving to the hills of Vermont had been to get closer to the land, I spent so much time working both at home and away that I hardly ever got outside to enjoy it. Memories of spending holidays and vacations here as a kid were filled with endless outdoor fun where the back hill called to us at all times of day and night for walking, sledding, tobogganing, and cross-country skiing. But within the precepts of my workaday marriage, a recreational walk was an unusual and solitary event. Afraid I might incur criticism from my husband, I assured myself the walk would be short.

Pulling on my parka and boots, I imagined a simple jaunt along the road which ran between the hundred-year-old farmhouse and barn, across the valley floor, over a bridge over a stream, and up a steep hill. A storm the night before had dumped a load of fresh snow and as I stepped out the kitchen door, I could see a few oversized flakes still drifting down.

I bounded off the porch to the road. In winter, it was plowed only to the barn and was otherwise closed. Sinking into a snowdrift up to my thighs, my walk soon turned to a trudge, my strides barely half a boot long. My steps, steady and rhythmic, set a tempo for my thoughts. The frenzied pace of holiday preparations gave way. I settled into my body, enveloped as it was in heavy clothing, and made my way along the valley floor in the soft, deep, white.

At the bridge, the road became a ski-mobile track. My boots now crunched on a hard-packed surface. Over the bridge I continued along the road as it climbed the hill.

About halfway up, I came upon a familiar old logging path now used as a deer corridor cutting across the slope on my right. It extended up into the woods as a slight depression under the new snowfall. Filled with an urge to follow it, I stopped. It meant reentering the depths of the snow. It meant not sticking to my plan for a short walk up and back down the road. Curiosity nudged me forward. It looked so inviting....

I gave in.

On the logging path, trudge mode took over again. I relaxed my shoulders and, entertained by the whzz-whzz from my parka, let my arms swing gently at my sides. With no goal, no expectation, contentment filled me. I looked up to watch the snow-laden branches pass overhead. I looked around at the snow-bent briars and bushes, admiring their beauty.

When I came upon a stand of white pine trees I wanted to step toward them. Off the logging path. *Into even deeper snow?* I mused but didn't hesitate. In contrast to the hardworking, focused identity I typically prided myself in, the curiosity, the impulsive behavior, the suspended sense of self, all were truly odd.

Well, now what? I wondered.

I was urged to go over to one of the trees. When I did I was overwhelmed: its girth easily dwarfed my outstretched arms. Pressing my nose to the bark, its furrows appeared as high ridges and deep valleys. How many times had I come this way and never really seen this tree? Leaning my head way back to look into its crown, I walked a reverent circle around its base.

A new impulse beckoned me away from the tree. I responded fluidly, pressing a mittened palm on its trunk as I turned, I knew not where. My glance was arrested at the trunk of another tree and the impulse said *Yes*. This one was on top of a short, steep hummock resulting in several missteps. When finally level with the base of the tree I saw that its trunk curved away from the hill and twisted around all the way to the top. Although it appeared frozen in time, static and still, deep inside of me I could feel its powerful force, an eternal dance, flowing and spiraling.

I placed two mittened palms on the trunk and shared a moment of deep connection. And then I turned to go. No sooner had I formed a *Where?* in my mind then another impulse had me, this time following a curving route which ran very deliberately between two young beech trees, under a bending bough, around an igloo shaped thicket.

For a while I wandered in a magic spell. I don't remember for how long, or exactly what I encountered, but the discoveries and wonders never ceased. I chuckled and chattered to myself, ever increasing my amazement and disbelief. I didn't pay any attention to where I was going. When I paused and looked back I saw that my footprints had made a winding, twisting dance of their own in the snow.

Where to from here? I thought.

An impulse beckoned me down into a hollow filled with a fallen tree. I resisted. It looked like a dead end. Everywhere else I had been led had flowed in continuous motion. I looked around and waited for what I hoped would be a more appropriate impulse. Nothing. I looked again at the fallen tree and thought, *There? Really?* The pull was unmistakable. I shrugged, trudging down until I came right up to it. It lay about waist high so I couldn't just step over it. Underneath lay a tangle of dead branches. I couldn't go under it, either.

"Now what?" I asked out loud, I admit, somewhat belligerently. The silent directive was strong and clear: I was to climb onto it. Not over it, but onto it. "Okay," I muttered, pulling myself up.

"So now I'm supposed to stand up or something?" Of course I was, and so I did.

Whether by coincidence or design I stood facing outwards, my back to the hill. And there, through a small break in the canopy, perfectly framed by the boughs of several hemlock trees, way down in the valley below, was my house. From that particular vantage point up on that fallen tree I could see nothing else of the valley, neither north, nor south, nor east, nor west, nothing except that singular telescopic view. I stood stunned, enveloped in something larger than life, a feeling beyond knowing.

"Is this for real?" Was all I could muster after a few jaw-dropping moments. I looked around me, and again at my house in its custom frame. All very real.

What I couldn't have known then, nor even understood until nearly forty years later, was that in that moment I was being offered a glimpse, a glimmer, a tiny window of perspective on the intention I had set long ago, inspired by my Folklore and the Supernatural class to expand my experience of reality and the unrecognized life that awaited me. Powers at work, far beyond understanding, would eventually take me a long way, not so much geographically but psychically and spiritually, from both the family vacation home that had fashioned me, and the confines of the marriage within it which presently defined my days.

"Okay," I said out loud. "What next?"

I was cookin' now, ready for anything, and at the same time fully expecting this inexplicable dance to dissipate and shrink back to an ordinary walk on an ordinary day, where I would be left with nothing more than an uncertain memory and maybe a good story to tell. But it didn't stop there at all. I was led through another maze of natural wonders, pausing only now and then to look back at the winding trail I left behind. At length I arrived at what I immediately recognized to be the end of the journey: A couple of otherwise unremarkable thorn apple trees created a shrine in front of me, their branches arching gracefully into the snow, white on white, white into white, each twig, each thorn a crystalline jewel in this humble crown. Awkwardly I knelt, my knees cushioned, my mind quiet and my heart full.

"Thank you," I said, I guess partly to the trees for their beauty, and partly to whatever or whoever had brought me here and invited me to enter this world. I remained there leaning comfortably on the heels of my big boots with my mittens resting on the surface of the snow.

And then, I was ready to go.

I stood up and said a silent *Goodbye*. As I left, I walked in straight lines, first to find the logging path, and then to follow it back to the main road, decidedly self-directed. I hastened forward, back in ordinary time, worrying once again about what my husband might be thinking. Sensing a tenuous connection to whatever I had found, I encased the magic, fiercely and privately, deep within, fearing I would lose it altogether if I tried to interpret or explain. This winter walk had both embodied and transcended my dormant dreams. In a land of winter slumber, they had awakened inside of me again

CHAPTER SIX

Wild Turkey Trot

*"The Turkey... is a symbol of all the blessings that
the Earth contains, along with the ability to use
them to their greatest advantage."*

—-Ted Andrews, *Animal-Speak*

FALL, 1986

WITH A NEW JOB situation, which included woodworking full-time and waitressing on weekends, life got a little
easier. A welcome relief. With that lighter frame of mind, I
set out for a walk one fall afternoon after work still in my
sawdusty brown corduroys, tan shop boots, and black zip-
pered sweatshirt. I crossed the bridge and was starting to
feel the slight incline of the hill in my now often fatigued
body and strained breathing. As I rounded the sharp curve
that always bedeviled us tobogganing as kids, and really
started to climb I was winded almost instantly. I slowed
down by taking shorter steps, and leaned my hands alternately against my thighs for added strength.

My colors blended with the grays, browns, and blacks around me. November in rural Vermont was washed out and bleak, often cold and wet, but thankfully not that day. Partway up the first stretch of the big hill, I heard a vague sort of rustle from the woods below to my left. When I stopped to listen, it became a light, though distinct, and rhythmic crunch-crunch, crunch-crunch, crunch-crunch, crunch-crunch.... I peered into the woods, homing in on the source of the sound, but saw nothing at first. Then I spotted them, a little below eye-level and about 100 feet away: two sets of long skinny trotting legs, two long necks reaching out beyond mottled brown and black feathered bodies, heads glancing from side to side in minute arcs as if to see behind them. Aside from the sound and the motion, they were indistinct from their surroundings. I was thankful for the dry, windless weather. I listened and watched as they crested a rounded hummock and disappeared down the other side. I could still hear them, crunch-crunch, crunch-crunch, crunch-crunch, crunch-crunch, so I waited. Sure enough they re-emerged, crested another mound and disappeared again. I listened and watched them appear and disappear until they had passed my visual horizon where the forest floor curved into the dark, tangled, leafless canopy.

I resumed my walk up the hill. *Turkeys, wow!* I had been hearing about them at work. In some parts of Vermont you could hunt them, but not here. Apparently, they were very shy and elusive and not often seen. Happy for the fleeting moment, I continued walking, still hearing the *crunch-crunching* in my mind. Upon reaching the top of the road's first steep ascent, I enjoyed the now more level surface. With my body warmed and my muscles primed, I seemed to float along. The road straightened for a time and then curved to the left in the beginning of a large S. As I reached its center and the road began to rise, I heard a single twig snap and glanced up ahead of me to where the road wrapped back around the hill to the right. A small shoulder of the hill met the road at this point and, along with a medium-sized beech tree, blocked any further view.

Up over the outer embankment of the road popped a turkey and as it trotted lightly across another appeared, following the first. As the second was crossing and the first disappearing behind the beech tree and shoulder, up popped another, and as that one was crossing and the second was disappearing up popped another. Their movements and formation were even, regular, measured. The birds were swift without being hurried, sure and precise. They reminded me of cardboard ducks on a conveyor belt at a shooting gallery, and I counted six in all. Other than the snap of that first twig, they were completely silent. After I saw the last one disappear, and convinced they must be huddling on the other side of that shoulder, I ran as quickly and silently as I could to reach the curve. As I rounded it to get a closer look at them, I was rewarded only with a barren, empty gully. I couldn't believe my eyes. *They were just here!* I looked through the trees up the hill and listened, sure that if they were scurrying away I would see or hear them. I had to, they were right here! But there was nothing. No sound, no movement, and no obvious hiding places. It was as if they had disappeared into thin air.

Truly perplexed, I even entertained a moment of doubt about having seen them at all. But that was ridiculous! I knew I had. Shaking my head, I turned back to the road and headed on up the hill. At this juncture it became very steep, the steepest yet. I was hardly aware of the climb. My thoughts were steeped in turkey musings: *but how?... but where?... but they were ... and I was ... it didn't take me that long to ...* vain thoughts hammering. I couldn't make any sense of it. After another rigorous climb the road leveled out and emerged from the woods. There was a hayfield on my left and as I walked it got bigger and bigger. The road started to rise again and when I looked back over my shoulder I could begin to see a magnificent view of the valley below.

I decided to continue on up to my neighbor's sheep farm. That way I would have climbed all the steepest parts of the ridge for the exercise. As I crested the last shoulder of the hill I saw my neighbor crossing the road from his barn back towards the house. He crooked his elbow and gave a single wave with his left hand. I waved back, and yelled, "Hello!" He stopped. I increased my pace until I'd caught up to him. We smiled and exchanged pleasantries about the weather, the walk, his sheep. I told him about the turkeys and he said, "Yeah, they're around here all right. I haven't seen them too much, though." We chatted some more and then parted.

Heading down hill took on an energy all its own and I had to hold back my now wobbling legs against the gravitational pull of the road's pitch. This seemed to cause my arms to swing wildly as if they were releasing the energy my legs were holding back. I felt like a Raggedy Ann doll, and it made me laugh. When I came to the Turkey Shoulder curve in the road, I peered intently up into the woods again to wonder. I was feeling kind of silly and free when I came upon the road's last steep decline, almost skipping, but not really.

"Ahhhuuuuuuuuupgupgupgupgup," called from out of the woods to my left, sounding halfway between a croak and a screech, though not very loud.

"Ahhhuuuuuuuuuuuuuupgupgupgup," came again, and as I stopped to look around and up, I saw two big birds take flight from two trees. They descended in a straight forty-five degree line and landed, stirring up a squawking, speckled commotion on the forest floor. As I watched, totally dumbstruck, a dozen or so wild turkeys began to trot wildly, crunch-crunch, crunch-crunch, crunch-crunch, crunch-crunch, at first weaving to and fro and bumping into one another other until, straightening out, they formed a loose but orderly crew and disappeared up the hill.

When quiet returned to the forest floor, I continued to stare, mentally pinching myself in disbelief. The turkeys' journey that afternoon seemed somehow inextricably interwoven with my own. In the space of perhaps an hour, they had revealed their reclusive selves to me in three distinct glimpses, each one closer and more intimate than the last. Looking back, it was as if there was something they wanted me to see. Now that I appreciate St. Francis's revelation that nature mirrors the Divine, I realize that the encounter couldn't have been more prescient. And while all of this makes surprising sense as to how my life continued to unfold, increasingly guided by Earth-based spirituality, at the time this insight would have seemed at best curious, more likely vague and abstract.

In that moment, I did something rather more down-to-earth.

"Eaaaaaaaaaaapgipgipgipgip," I half croaked, half squeaked quietly to myself. *Nope.* I tried again. "Ahhhuuuuuuuuuuupgupgupgup." Yeah, that was it.

"Ahhhuuuuuuuuuuupgupgupgup!" I wanted to remember the call. Just in case I ever got a chance to tell this story, I wanted to get it right.

CHAPTER SEVEN

Troubled Waters

"We live in a relational space that is real in every sense. It is meaningful, alive, and tangible. It permeates us, and it connects us, and it is us."

—Jeff Carreira, *The Soul of a New Self*

SPRING, 1987

MY HUSBAND AND I bought our first house several miles up a dirt road in central Vermont. Having moved north from Pennsylvania three years earlier to share a dream of a back-to-the-land lifestyle rich with woodworking, organic gardening, and folk music, and now having endured three long, cold Vermont winters, each one on a mere two-and-a-half cords of firewood which we had sourced, felled, chain-sawed, hauled, split, stacked, and dried ourselves, we figured we had tested our "flatlander" mettle and proved worthy to take this next step. Through my multiple jobs, collaborative do-it-yourself efforts, and serious scrimping we had amassed our downpayment, plus some additional funds for much-needed improvements.

Our purchase included an old farmhouse, which had been used as a hunting camp for many years, a listing barn, and a generous number of acres of mostly wooded land. Angular, ledgy, and wild, this land's restless spirit was expressed by the constant sound of rushing water. Most prominently, at a medium to high pitch, was a little brook that marked the southern boundary of our property. It ran down from a series of springs seeping out from the steep ledge behind our house, resounding with intimate gurgles and irregularities. Deeper in the background was the steady, muted rumble of a creek, the moderately-sized but aggressive sculptor of this elevated valley. Its path straight and pitched, it had no patience or tolerance for silt and sand but rather kept its crystal clear water in a constant scour against an unyielding bed of pebbles and stones.

We loved the idea of being so far out of town in the outback. Somewhat frantic about the enormity of the tasks that lay ahead, we took up residence in early summer. My priorities included maintaining our income through a woodworking job by day and waitressing by night; shopping for food, working at our local co-op, cooking, cleaning, and hauling drinking water. And somehow finding time to do our laundry in town during my lunch break. My husband's priorities all related to making the house livable for winter: hooking up the wood stove; gathering firewood; plugging holes to discourage the critters that had been making the house their home; and keeping water flowing into our indoor plumbing from its source in a submerged handmade box in the stream behind our house through more than a hundred yards of unprotected pipe.

One evening later that summer, I took a brief moment to go out on the porch and breathe in the energy and essence of this new place, little knowing how complex and changeable my relationship with its waters was to become over the next year. As I stood there with my face raised to the night sky, inviting the sounds to wash through me, suddenly I heard a distinct though distant CRACK! followed by CRACK! CRACK! CRACK! and then a long CRAAAAAAAAAAACK! ending with a THUD! A tree falling, obviously. I went inside to mention it to my husband.

"It's probably just an old rotten one," he responded, and neither of us gave it much thought until the same thing happened a few nights later. The following day when arriving home after work, I spotted him by the side of the narrow road a little ways down from our house and pulled to a stop beside him. I rolled down the window and he delivered the bad news.

"We have beaver," he said solemnly. He gestured behind him toward the creek which cut its way through a ten-acre field in a floodplain below the road. "They've cut down two healthy poplar trees along the bank!" He sounded indignant. "And look here," he said, moving off to the side revealing several tooth marks in a good-sized poplar behind him. I had a sinking feeling inside, more from the alarm in his voice than anything else.

"Wow," was all I said.

A week passed, filled with its usual frenzy of activity, the beavers almost forgotten. But another day after work my husband met me with more bad news. "They're building a dam. They're trying to dam the creek!"

"Really?" I said as I stepped from the truck. I was excited, amazed, and concerned, wondering what it meant for the beavers, for the trees, and for us. My husband led me down through the field to the riverbank, while telling me that he had spent all day trying to break the dam and that he had finally succeeded. As I struggled across a mucky area tangled with alders I noticed it was strangely quiet. The creek's familiar roar had become more of a hiss. When I emerged from the scrub I saw why. In front of me stretched a twenty foot dam, completely spanning the stream except for a small opening against the opposite bank where a narrow band of water poured through in a taffy-like twist. The four-foot-high barrier of branches, small logs, and sticks acted like a sieve, not completely stopping the water but controlling it, harnessing it, squeezing it through a few small holes, but forcing it primarily out from underneath, where with less vigor it roiled and churned, and then continued on its way in a gaping, half-empty riverbed.

I looked up in surprise when my husband climbed onto it and walked out along the dam's narrow and uneven ridge. He caught my look of alarm.

"Don't worry," he half-laughed with a little testing jump. "It's solid."

I climbed up on it, too. Boy, was it ever! The upstream side I could now see had been packed with mud and orange, yellow, and red leaves. The level of the water looked about halfway up.

"The water's dropped about a foot," he said. I didn't know what to say. He started talking and pointing, but it took me a few moments to give him my full attention.

"... and there's their lodge." He was pointing upstream.

"Where?" I asked. He came up next to me and extended his arm out from my eye level, pointing hard. Then I could see a seemingly haphazard mound of sticks brimming above the still water.

My husband was very concerned about the trees. He loved trees. As a boy he had taken great pride in planting some in his yard, which, twenty years later he pointed out to me during a deliberate drive by his old neighborhood. As a teenager he had frequented a nearby arboretum and collected hickory nuts. "You had to go out at just the right time," he told me, "because if you got there too late the squirrels would get 'em all. They all kind of fall at once." And he loved wood: his dream for the last ten years or so had been to build handmade acoustic guitars. Before that, he had dreamed of being a carpenter. So, naturally, it was the wood that worried him now.

"Here," my husband said, bending down to grab onto a branch. "Let's see if we can pull this apart some more. It'll go faster with two of us." I hesitated. I was fascinated by the dam. But out of loyalty and deference to my husband, I kept silent. Not with a whole lot of enthusiasm, I bent down and, reaching with two hands, I wrapped my fingers around a cold, wet, blackened branch and started to pull. Nothing. I pulled harder. Still nothing. I tried pushing and twisting the branch and was only able to get it to move an inch or so. I soon fell into a rhythm of yanking, pushing, twisting, prying, and then pulling again, gradually increasing its range of movement, realizing that the dam was no simple pile of sticks. It had been expertly crafted, with the knobs, curves, crooks, and Y's of each stick deliberately interlocked with those of the others. When finally I got the branch to give way, it came out only a foot or so before it hooked again. Getting it all the way out was a long process, and I must admit, not a very satisfying one. After about an hour, my husband and I had managed to open the gap at the far end just a little more, and we stood back to watch a now slightly wider twist of dark water pour through.

"Well, I'm beat!" he announced. I agreed. "The water level's really dropping now," he continued, sounding relieved. With my new respect for the genius and craftsmanship of the beaver, I ached dully at the satisfaction in his voice. We withdrew from the dam and headed back up through the field to our house.

The next day when I returned from work my husband was not at the house. On a hunch, I headed down to the dam. I found him there, once again hard at work.

"Hey, there," I called, and waved. He stopped and looked up.

"I'm almost done," he called back. "I'll be up in a little while!"

Later, over dinner, he told me that the hole we had made was repaired overnight, but that it wasn't as strong and came apart more easily today. So, he had spent most of the day making it bigger, to make it harder for the beaver to repair. Over the next few weeks my husband waged a daily war on the beaver dam. And each night, his unseen foes repaired it. I was inwardly conflicted. Battle weary, I wished he would leave the beavers alone. At the same time, I didn't want to lose all our trees.

Finally, he called a wildlife ranger to come out and take a look.

"Looks to me like they're going to try to flood the whole lower end here," said the Forester with a sweep of his hand after we had led him out into the field. "You see over there," he continued, pointing towards the embankment with the road, "they have another natural hill. If they build the dam all the way across your field they could have themselves quite a pond." He paused. "But you know, I don't think it's deep enough for them here. I don't think they'll stay the winter. If the water's not deep enough for them around their lodge, they'll freeze."

"And if they do stay," started my husband, "you think they'll dam all the way across the field?"

"It's possible."

"And just keep taking down trees?"

"Yeah, they would do that," said the ranger nodding. "You see, they only eat the very tops of the trees, and they especially like poplar."

"What can we do?" I asked.

"Well you can do what you're doing, keep trying to discourage them, or—"

"Or what?" asked my husband.

"Well, as landowners you're entitled to have them trapped." In the silence that ensued, I felt the weight of land ownership suddenly settle heavily upon my shoulders and heart.

My husband and the beavers seemed to be at a stalemate. Each was equally determined. Finally, the threat of winter fast approaching called him away from the dam and back to pressing tasks. Meanwhile, the dam secured, the beavers proceeded to build up an embankment around the outside of the burgeoning pond and gathered tree tops to feed on in the winter months. The bases of all the trees which had lined the riverbank were now under water. A smooth layer of ice formed behind the dam and soon all was draped in white.

My husband and I continued to discuss the beavers. We reluctantly decided that we would contact a trapper. I was to actually make the call, because I worked in town, and could make it locally from there. The next day, I dialed from a pay phone outside a gas station just north of town, my breath steaming into the receiver. They guy seemed a little doubtful, because he wasn't sure if their furs would still be worth it. He said he'd charge us twenty dollars, just in case. I said okay and explained to him where we lived. I jammed the phone down hard in its cradle, feeling defeated and numb.

About a week later we saw some tracks leading down to the pond. We never heard anything from the guy though, so after about a month, at my husband's urging, I called him up again. I was hoping maybe he'd forgotten.

"Yup. I pulled two beavers from your pond, a male and a female. That was a while ago, wasn't it?" he said. I agreed, thanked him numbly and hung up.

My husband and I never discussed our feelings. I grieved for a long time, burdened by guilt. As before, we just let the whole thing alone, hoping, I think, that it was now behind us. I walked down there once toward the end of winter and enjoyed the stillness. There were no tracks, no signs of activity.

SPRING 1988. AFTER A long, hard winter, longer daylight and brighter sunshine began to thaw the land. Spring was slow and cautious, but by the middle of May the snow was completely gone from the hayfield, and by the beginning of June it was adorned with bright emerald grass jeweled with wildflowers. At the same time, the trees leafed out. My husband and I didn't talk about the drowned trees surrounding the pond.

One day later that month I walked down through the hayfield for no particular reason. The dead grasses from previous seasons pricked the bottom of my bare feet, while the tips of the new grass tickled my shins and calves. I soon found myself standing at the edge of the beaver pond, drawn again by its stillness in contrast to the rapidly moving water everywhere else. The water was dark and murky with a heavy, unpleasant smell. Suddenly, a movement on the pond's surface caught my eye. I squinted and stepped closer. There, all the way against the far bank, I spotted a fuzzy little brown duckling paddling around. Then there was another, and another and another! Pretty soon I had counted six, and continued to watch as, obviously aware of me now, they huddled together protectively and swam nervously first one way and then, turning abruptly, back the other way.

I stood, transfixed and entranced, and watched. Suddenly I heard a call of alarm from high over my shoulder. I looked up to see what I assumed to be a mother duck swooping down to her brood. I studied her markings so I could look her up in our bird book. She led them quickly onto the opposite bank where they disappeared behind a tree. I turned back to the house, musing. *A family of ducks nesting on our beaver pond.*

The distinctive swept-back crest and bright contrasting colors made the duck easy to identify, except that she turned out to be a he. "Hey, honey," I called when I heard him come up on the porch. "We have wood ducks nesting on the beaver pond! I saw six little ones and a father just now."

"Wood ducks. Wow," he responded politely. He liked birds a lot, but he liked trees even more, and the beaver pond was still a sensitive subject. Somewhat deflated by his lack of enthusiasm, I pictured again those little ducklings in my mind. I realized, perhaps for the first time, that the pond presented the potential for an entirely new ecosystem in these rugged parts. I silently thanked, and apologized to, the beavers and decided to make peace with their legacy.

After that, I tried to visit the pond as often as I could. I never did see the ducks again. I figured that, because they were still too young to fly, they must have been watching out for me and staying out of sight. But there was always plenty of activity down there, with songbirds, chipmunks, and squirrels. One particularly warm and sunny day in July I decided to stop by a tree at the water's edge, a little way upstream from the pond. With the ten-foot-wide tributary in front of me, I sat cross-legged and gazed into the quiet, clear water to the muddy bottom where I could just make out a few pieces of debris drifting by slowly.

Suddenly, a ripple in the water's surface impeded my view and I looked around for the source. Nothing. Then, a distinct "splash" from upstream brought my head around to the right and there, not twenty feet from where I sat, was a young beaver. She was playing on a log on the muddy bank. Despite my excitement and disbelief I froze, hoping I would be able to watch, unnoticed. But in the same moment the little critter looked up, directly at me it seemed, and then turned and scurried back into the stream.

Damn! I thought as I continued to gaze in disappointment at the spot where she disappeared. I guessed she sensed me. The sound of water rippling brought my gaze back directly in front of me where I just caught sight of the little beaver underwater swimming past. I was amazed to have caught one last glimpse. Much to my surprise, she swam beyond me only a few feet before turning around and coming back. She remained just below the water's surface, on her side, facing me with what, I swear, looked like a mischievous little grin. Again, she stopped only a few feet beyond me and turned around. This time when she swam back she stopped right in front of me. With just the top half of her head out of water, she regarded me with two very dark eyes.... Mesmerized, I returned her gaze.

Our hypnotic communion was interrupted suddenly by a loud THWAP! from downstream. I whipped around to look. THWAP! came the slap of a beaver's tail again as a fat and furry brown back curled and disappeared under water. I turned back to look for the little one but she was gone. Soon I saw the much larger shape of the adult beaver underwater wiggling past, hugging the bottom of the stream. I watched it for as long as I could and then continued to follow its approximate progress. A safe distance upstream the adult resurfaced and slapped its tail again. Meanwhile, the little one appeared in front of me again and, ignoring the parent's warning, rolled back and forth from her belly to her back, looking at me the entire time.

The adult dove under again and pretty soon I could see it skimming the bottom. This time it surfaced a safe distance downstream. THWAP! THWAP! THWAP! went its tail several times, with a dive after each one. Then it was gone. The little one had also disappeared and didn't come back.

I sat for a while as the familiar stillness returned to the pond, amazed and perplexed. *Did the trapper lie? Or did he go to the wrong place? Or had there been four adults? Or did this family just move in?* Somehow, none of it made sense. The image of that playful little beaver affixing me with her gaze stirred something tender within, thawed something frozen. Somehow, out of a multitude of wrongs, something sweet and dear had come forth. Watery dreams flowed forth as a pond with new life. An adorable, trusting little furry being sought me out to play. A family of four-legged woodworkers had been trying to make a new home just as we had been trying to make ours.

It was incomprehensible.

I mentioned none of these liminal musings to my husband.

One afternoon about a month later I was in the kitchen doing dishes when I heard my husband calling my name from outside. I reached for the dish towel but before I could finish drying my hands he was at the screen door.

"Katy," he began, breathlessly. "You have to come see this. There are two great blue herons down at the beaver pond. C'mon. Hurry."

"Okay, okay, I'm coming!" I replied, balling up the dish towel and throwing it on the counter. I hurried across the kitchen, wiping my hands on my pants, and stepped out onto the porch. As he gestured for quiet, I eased the screen door closed behind me.

"I saw them first way off in the distance," he started in hushed tones as we descended the porch steps and hurried down toward the pond, "but I couldn't tell what they were. As they got closer I thought they might be heron but I couldn't figure out what they'd be doing so far up in the hills. When they were almost overhead they swooped down into the trees over the pond. Oh, boy," he whispered excitedly, "from this close they look like they're moving in slow motion … they're so beautiful!" He paused, and then went on. "Anyway, it's the first time it's really sinking in that we have a pond here, at least enough of one to catch their attention."

When we got to the alder thicket, he put out his hand in caution and we both slowed down. Just then, with a great commotion of flapping wings and snapping branches, the two herons took off. My husband and I watched the graceful birds return to flight, as if in slow motion, just as he had said. He reached out and took my hand and together we squinted up in silence until the birds disappeared over the eastern ridge. This divine gift from the beavers is my sweetest memory of our years together.

The beavers stayed well into the fall of that year. We left them alone but kept tabs on any new happenings down at the pond. By the time winter set in the beavers had abandoned their lodge and dam and moved on. All winter the dam remained intact, snow covered and silent. But when the spring floods and ice jams broke through, the muddy waters of the pond drained away, and the brook again ran clear and free, leaving only a ring of dead trees.

CHAPTER EIGHT

Harmonic Convergence

"Consciousness is a living field of life energy that permeates the cosmos and provides a reflective capacity for material forms at every scale throughout the universe."

—Duane Elgin, *The Living Universe*

SUMMER, 1987

ONE DAY AT MY woodworking job I heard a reference on National Public Radio to a spiritual event happening out in Colorado. My curiosity piqued, I called the radio station to get more information. I talked with a woman who could tell me only that the event was called the Harmonic Convergence. That night at my waitress job I dared to mention it to a fellow waitress who shared an interest in New Age phenomena but with whom I had never until now connected comfortably. As it turned out she knew about the event and even offered to photocopy all the information she had and bring it in to work for me. I was touched.

The following day she delivered several articles in which I later read that this Harmonic Convergence was being recognized and celebrated all over the world. Apparently, it related to ancient Mayan and Aztec calendars which had marked the upcoming date, August 17, 1987 (8/17/87), as a turning point for the Earth, when it would enter a new phase of greater enlightenment. The readings recommended that those interested should celebrate in groups if possible, but if not, then with a simple sunrise salute. I found out the next day that my colleague and her boyfriend were intending to celebrate by camping in the Adirondack Mountains. Since I didn't know anyone else interested, I decided to celebrate on my own.

On the morning of Sunday, August 17, 1987, I awoke to the alarm at 4:00 a.m. and arose in total darkness. I wanted to experience the very first light of day break upon the land. Since I lived in a high narrow valley running north/south between two higher ridges, I had decided that I would climb up the steep hill behind my house to an abandoned hayfield where I could better see the sun rise over the eastern ridge. I dressed quickly and grabbed some food to bring along.

With much uncertainty and trepidation I stepped out of the house to enter the darkness of this early morning world. I could see the corner of night turning to twilight as I climbed initially through a small field behind the house. At the top of the field, shadowed trees loomed up in front of me. My heartbeat quickened, pumping an aching wave of adrenalin through my limbs. I crashed loudly through the outer vegetative layer, wanting, I think, to appear more powerful than I felt to those dark unknowns lurking within. I continued to push forward, partially stooped, my arms stretched protectively out in front of me, snapping crisp conifer twigs and branches, scrambling up slippery moss-covered rocks—anxious to reach the top safely, anxious to be present for this experience, anxious to share my energy with the cosmos, anxious, anxious, anxious.

As I climbed, my surroundings changed from black to blue and, by the time I reached the abandoned field, to grey: blue-grey, green-grey, and the yellow-grey of goldenrod. After just a few short steps into the field of waist-high grass and shrubs my pants, wet, cold, and heavy, were sucking down on my thighs, and in my shoes bubbles of water squished and squeaked through my toes. I held my arms out to my sides, hands facing down, fingers stretched, and let the tips of the tall vegetation tickle my palms. I felt awkward and self-conscious, but committed, nevertheless.

Step by step I traversed the gently sloping five-acre field to the highest point along its western border. Then, I turned to face the dawn. Red, pink, salmon, orange, yellow; a glow, a spark, a streak, a shimmer, a sliver, a slice, a crescent, a quarter, a half, three quarters, a whole. Burning through grey, burning through air, through sky, through cosmic abyss. Burning through time, creating time, creating everything. The light entered my consciousness, millions of molecules from millions of miles away, with me now for the present, a moment defined by us together.

With the sunlight came a wall of hot, heavy air. I stood, and looked to the sky, stretching out my arms as far as I could, as if to embrace everything. And then I danced. The articles had said this would be an opportunity for Sun Children to re-awaken to themselves and their true nature, to become leaders in the dawn of a new world, a new era, a new reality. I felt like a child of the sun: full and round and alive. I also felt small, and alone, and frightened. *Me? A leader?* I thought. *I don't know*. I would have liked to think so. But it scared me.

This was the first time I had ever consciously sought to act on my growing conviction that reality is bigger and more mysterious than the Western scientific paradigm in which I had been acculturated had led me to believe. I entered into the celebration fully expecting or hoping I would receive some kind of outside confirmation for my beliefs: A space-ship from the great beyond would be nice—if somewhat terrifying. There was nothing like that. It was an ordinary morning on an ordinary day. What was extraordinary was my behavior and my intense attunement to the sun's rising. It is only now as I write these words that I fully appreciate that. In fact, it occurs to me that reality is actually quite ex-traordinary, even everyday ordinary reality. How we choose to experience it is what matters. It can be tediously unre-markable, or forever wonderful. And I am forever full of wonder.

CHAPTER NINE

Reciprocity

*"At that moment when each thing, each event pres-
ents itself again as a psychic reality, then I am held
in an enduring intimate conversation with matter."*

—James Hillman,
The Thought of the Heart and the Soul of the World

FALL, 1987

ON A COOL, DRY September afternoon I took a walk
up into those same woods I had gone crashing through a
month earlier on the morning of the Harmonic Convergence. This time though I stayed down by the stream that
was fed by several springs further up the hill, carving its
way in a gully that ran straight up to that abandoned hayfield. While walking along thinking about nothing in particular except how good it felt to be alone in these woods,
suddenly out of the corner of my eye I *saw* the personality
of a big, old hemlock tree.

What do I mean? I mean that I had a visual impression of
a wrinkled elder emerging from the folds and crags of the

bark and branches, while simultaneously sensing the presence of a wise old sage. I felt its salutation, as if it had called to me. Stunned, I walked up to the tree, put my hand gently on the bark, and smiled. I may have said "Hello" but I don't remember. I stayed there for a couple of minutes, looking curiously up into its crown. Then I left.

As I continued up the hill I awakened to a whole new world. I was wide-eyed and alert. I looked about me with this new vision and encountered many tree personalities that day: old, young, serious, playful, wizened, and naive. And ever since, I have continued to do this. It's as if, while the center of my gaze projects my own mental energy outward, the periphery receives energy inwards. It is always through the corner of my eye that I first receive a salutation, that I am called by a tree. But then I can look directly at it and still experience the personality and the message.

While I am more comfortable with this now, at the time I lacked a context for it. It seemed closely connected to my dances with the trees on a snowy hillside a couple of years before, and it occurred to me then that perhaps all those impulses I followed had come from the trees. Perhaps even this was why I had had that moment in college thinking like an oak tree. Curious but still bewildered, I kept it all to myself. My secret world.

On another day I went out to pick apples. When we had moved to this new home, we discovered some old apple trees on the property which had been overgrown with brush. We didn't even really know they were there at first, but after a bit of excavation they emerged in all their ancient splendor. We didn't prune them or spray them. I didn't even pick the apples directly from their branches but instead gathered them off the ground. Invariably, they were slightly bruised or mottled or deformed. But there was such an abundance it never mattered. I cut out the bad spots and still had plenty left over for cooking and freezing.

On this day I decided to acknowledge the trees before I began, and to thank them when I was through. For some reason, it just felt right. There were two trees in particular which bore tasty and generally healthy fruit. As I approached the first tree, which my husband and I had named "Amanda," I smiled and spoke to her. I offered my humble appreciation and danced a little, attempting to mimic her sweeping grace in my improvised movements. Then I shook open the first paper bag and began to pick through the fallen apples.

Pretty soon the repetition of stooping, reaching, grasping, inspecting, and depositing became fairly automatic and my thoughts began to drift. Suddenly, a distinct Thud! from somewhere behind snapped me out of my reverie. I spun around immediately and walked toward the sound, searching intently. I had never had an apple fall to the ground in my presence and it excited me.

There it was. As soon as I picked it up I knew this was no ordinary apple. First of all, it was big and round and perfectly formed—not a single blemish or wormhole. As I turned it over in my hand its skin color blended from yellow-gold to salmon-pink and back to yellow-gold. My mouth watered instinctively as I imagined biting into its delicately sweet and juicy flesh. But I resisted. I gazed at it, wondering what would be good enough for this regal orb, what would do it justice? Certainly not eating it, nor cooking it either. I couldn't even imagine putting it in the bag with the others. Mystified, I pushed it into the soft front pocket of my sweatshirt. At least it would be safe there. Then, full of excitement and wonder, I continued gathering until I had picked over all the other apples under the tree. The bag was nearly full. I thanked Amanda, carried the bag into the kitchen, and moved my little harvesting operation up to the other tree.

The second tree we had named "Bittersweet" after the nature of its fruit: the flesh was sweet but the skin was tart, even bitter sometimes. I made my overtures and began my methodical gatherings and daydreaming, until … Thud!

I straightened up and spun around, already smiling. I could see the apple from where I stood. In three long strides I was standing over it. Shaking my head and muttering softly under my breath, I crouched down and gently cupped the apple in my hand, turning it over as I lifted it, allowing its cool weight to caress my fingers and palm. Another perfect apple: firm, round, a deep ruby red, with a slight hint of dusty rose. Again my mouth watered, even as my mind ran over the probabilities of this doubly good fortune. I kissed it, and then pushed it through the other opening of my sweatshirt pocket, burgeoning now with bounty.

As I continued gathering, hampered only slightly by my desire to protect my two precious charges, my mind was tangled about what to do: Nothing seemed appropriate, neither eating, cooking, nor even saving them. But what else was there? Then I got it. It came to me in the image of ceremony, of dance, a primal urge to celebrate the cycles, the gifts, the abundance, the spirit of generosity. I would make an offering. In gratitude, I would offer them both back to the Earth. The knot untangled in my head. I felt fuller and emptier at the same time. I felt sad about giving them up, and ecstatic that I'd been given this opportunity, insight, and honor.

I finished gathering the rest of the Bittersweet apples and carried the half-full bag to the kitchen. Then, with a hand in each pocket cradling the apples, I headed up the hill to the woods behind our house, my favorite place. I didn't know exactly where I was going but when I found it I knew: a circular ground cover of lush, green moss where a shaft of sunlight shone in through a small break in the canopy. I knelt, the cool dampness of the earth seeping through to my knees. I tugged an apple out of each pocket, and with my hands open, held them in front of me in a timeless gesture of supplication.

"Dear Mother," I began haltingly. "Creator ... thank you for your generous gifts ... thank you for these two gems ... thank you for this lesson. I offer them back to you now in the spirit of abundance ... that they may nourish you and enter the unending cycle of giving and receiving.... Thank you."

Leaning forward, I placed the apples on the ground under the large protective leaves of a mountain maple shrub. I sat back on my heels for a quiet moment or two before I stood, turned, and left without looking back. A couple of times in the next week I was tempted to go back and see what had become of the apple flesh, but I resisted because I wanted only to remember them in their perfection. In my mind, they are still there, the two of them, nestled together under the shrub, glowing a little bit and laughing and telling the amazing tale to any pixies or fairies or devas who will stop to listen, of how they came to be there, of the awkward young woman with the long brown braid who picked them up and put them in her soft, dark, fuzzy pocket and set them reverently here.

CHAPTER TEN

Drawing Down the Moon

"The essential myth of the Moon is the myth of transformation ... a visible symbol of hope, the light that shone in the darkness of the human psyche."

—Jules Cashford, *The Moon: Myth and Image*

SUMMER, 1988

OUR SECOND YEAR AT the new homestead, I was driving home late one hot summer night after a long 15- or 16-hour workday. Out of weariness, I hunched forward on the steering wheel, gripping it tightly as a way to focus and stay alert. The road curved back and forth up a flat, sparsely populated valley. Well past midnight, I was alone on the road. Not long after I passed the last town and headed into a dark stretch I became aware of a bright light flashing intermittently in my rear and side view mirrors. Without looking directly into the glass for confirmation, I assumed it was a set of bright lights from a vehicle to my rear which would soon overtake me.

When the flashes continued but no headlights actually came into view I thought to actually check the mirrors: no car. Puzzled, I continued driving, but now I was regularly checking the mirrors in order to decipher the mystery. Pretty soon I realized it must be the moon overhead, its bluish-white light somehow shining in through the hatchback window and reflecting in the rearview mirror. I leaned over to the passenger side to see if I could spot the culprit, not believing it could actually be so bright. But no matter how I stretched and twisted I still couldn't see it, only flashes of light. It was either too high—*or it isn't the moon! A spaceship, perhaps?* Hadn't I read a book years ago about an alien abduction on a lonely stretch of road in these parts? I immediately pulled over, just in case, and got out to take a look.

Of course it was the moon! A very bright, full moon.

"You!" I scorned. "You've been jerkin' me around a bit now, haven't ya?" This delivered in my poor attempt at a Vermont vernacular.

I got back in the car and pulled back onto the road. As I continued home I kept trying to recreate the flashing that had originally caught my attention. Strangely, it didn't happen again. But I was aware of the moon's light now, and her presence, and it occurred to me that she had been deliberately playing with me, taking advantage of my fatigue and lack of focus.

A promise I had made to the moon years before had seeded my desire to move to Vermont in the first place. Not long after we had met, my husband had given me a book called Drawing Down the Moon for my birthday. The author, Margot Adler, was a familiar public radio personality, and now I discovered an author, too. How could one life contain so much richness? The book described that since the beginning of time women would gather together to honor the rhythms of nature, in harmony with the cycles of the seasons and the moon. They were healers and wisdom seekers who danced to the beat of a different drum.

Deeply moved, I had started to look for the moon through the overlit haze of the metropolitan night sky. Upon finding her only dimly, I promised that one day I would live in a place where I could see her more clearly. After I had moved to the rural Vermont countryside, and on the rare occasions I took a walk outside at night, I was astonished to see that even just a sliver of moon could throw such light on the valley floor, easily illuminating both bare ground and the oft-present snow.

Still on my drive home, now lighter, happier, more awake, I continued on up the valley highway for another ten miles or so and then turned an acute right angle onto the dirt road which snaked its way along a small mountain valley carved by the rushing creek three miles up to our house. I wasn't thinking much about the moon at this point but as I approached a swimming hole about a mile before home, I found myself pulling over to stop in the tall grass. I cut the lights, killed the engine and yanked on the parking brake.

The darkness, the simultaneous silence and sonorous sounds of crickets and rushing water engulfed me. For a brief moment I slumped back on the car seat, allowing the hard vinyl of the headrest to support the back of my head. I knew I was there only for the moon. I knew because only the moon could have intercepted such a weary journey home. I felt her pulling me to leave fatigue behind, to yield to the call of the water.

I got out of the car and looked up. I knew what I had to do and turned toward the swimming hole. I was about twenty feet above where it formed at the base of a large culvert running under the road. Due to the tall grass and shrubs, I couldn't actually see the water from where I stood. But I could hear it. In spite of an inchoate inner fear and resistance, I stepped through the tall grass and managed to find precarious footing down a gully of sand and loose rocks where I emerged onto a rocky ledge about five feet above a glassy pool.

To my left, about fifteen feet away, the menacing black mouth of the culvert offered an unyielding dark muscle of water, twitching and flexing as it unleashed its power into the vacant pool below. I turned away from this uncertainty to face the moon. I knew I needed to bare myself to her completely, uncompromisingly. I undressed slowly, cautiously, listening, glancing, waiting, expecting, fearing the arrival of the evil intruder, the stalking rapist, the high school beer party, whoever or whatever I didn't want to catch me here in my vulnerability.

The unbroken fall of water lulled me to a near confidence and utmost determination. Somehow the night had softened. Naked and humbled, I stood with my face upturned to receive the moon's blue light. Its tender wash upon my skin quieted my fears. *What bliss! What freedom!* I thanked her. Then I turned and walked along the rocky ledge in a gradual descent to a pebbled shore at the water's edge. As I waded into the shallow water my feet curved and clung painfully to the irregular stones, sending aching, chilling, warning waves up to the rest of my being.

Gradually I stepped further and further in until water encircled my thighs. There I stopped. Somehow the uncertain dark and doom of the center of the pool was too much for me. Visions of malevolent unknowns sucked me under even as I stood outside their sinister grasp. Taking a deep breath in, I exhaled slowly while crouching down in the enveloping chill, the water crawling to my neck, my feet maintaining their iron grip on the stones below. Then, I shot up out of the water, my feet scrambling for shore. I retraced the path up to my clothes, dressed without drying, and feeling strangely off balance, pushed forward up the gully to my car. Before I got in I paused for a moment, now feeling safe and secure, to remember the ecstasy and freedom that lay beyond my persistent self consciousness and fear.

Transcend-Dance

"I share these things because I believe that human beings should remember how to behave in the world, that knowing the sacred in all things, without grandiosity or denigration, is crucial to human habitation of Earth."

—Stephen Harrod Buhner, *Sacred Plant Medicine*

CHAPTER ELEVEN

Communion

"After the one extravagant gesture ... the universe
has continued to deal exclusively in extravagances."

—Annie Dillard, *Pilgrim at Tinker Creek*

SUMMER, 1989

A SEQUENCE OF DISASTROUS events uprooted us from
our rough-and-tumble homestead only a year-and-a-half
after we had moved in. Following several months of virtual
homelessness, we moved back to my parents' farmhouse
when it unexpectedly became vacant. Aftershocks rever-
berated through our marriage, causing me to question the
unyielding workaholic pact between us and stirring a need
to explore new possibilities and adventures for our lives.
Perhaps turning thirty also afforded me unprecedented
boldness.

One such adventure found us camping at a Community
Living conference up in Canadian dairy-farming country.
Restless and needing space, I got into the habit of taking
solitary morning walks. It seemed that no matter where I

was or what I did or how I planned it I always saw the moment of the sun rise. I was never in the same place or in the same circumstances, never knew what time it was, and couldn't always see the sky, whether from clouds or mist.

One morning in particular I opened my eyes in total darkness. Sensing it wasn't the middle of night, I lay on my back in my sleeping bag and stared blindly into the unseen apex of our tent. Soon enough, I felt the night heave a great sigh as it expelled the first indigo light of day. I slithered quietly out of my bag, dressed, and unzipped my way out of the tent. Soon I was walking, this time out the driveway to the main road.

As I progressed along several miles of road, the unfolding light revealed a smooth quilted blanket of stratus clouds overhead. The land also was smooth, and gently rolling. I passed field after field outlined with stone walls. At one point, from a higher vantage point on the road, I found myself looking across a field and down into a depression where, through a grove of aspen trees, I saw a placid pond, uniformly grey as it perfectly reflected the overcast sky.

I felt very drawn to this pond so I stepped off the road, hopped over a ditch, surmounted the stone wall and crossed the field, descending toward the depression. Not until I had passed through the trees and come right up to the pond did it reveal itself to me truly as a low-lying field draped in mist. And not until I entered the field did I find the mist to be a sea of wave-like tendrils hovering motionless, just about chest-high. I walked tentatively into this dreamy scene thinking to lose myself for a while, but something in me was uncomfortable, and not sure I belonged.

I headed back toward the edge and was just about to continue back to the road when quite suddenly I had a very urgent internal plumbing emergency—a call of nature, if you will. *Better here, than back by the road*, I thought. I knew it wouldn't wait until I got all the way back to the community. So, I stepped into the grove of aspen trees and did what I had to do. When I was done, I stepped out of my protective cover just in time to see the wave-like tendrils turn to flames, glowing a fiery orange-yellow-gold, lighted by long thin rays of sunlight spilling over a distant horizon through a small opening between the ridge top and the uniform gray blanket of clouds.

I stood in awe and watched the water-flames come alive, writhing in a delicate but ecstatic dance of illumination and evaporation, consuming themselves completely within several short minutes. As the last ribbons of mist disappeared so too did the sunlight, the once lenient cloud cover now hugging the horizon in a tight, seamless line, and I stood looking upon a perfectly empty and ordinary field.

CHAPTER TWELVE

The Great Escape

"The careful observer can glimpse the seemingly impossible even with the unaided eye, a fact which forces one to prostrate oneself in adoration before the mysterious origin of all things."

—Goethe

FALL, 1989

ANOTHER WALK, AND ONE of my last from our now uninhabitable homestead. We had driven over from my parents' house to work on it. On the way over, I was sullen and silent. My growing perception was that for the last seven years I had been slaving away for my husband, apologizing for myself, trying to make up for an unending list of grievous shortcomings. And now I hated how my life felt like a prison. I hated the intractable work ethic that bound us. I hated the house we had bought, and moved (disastrously) onto a new foundation. I hated that after all those years, all those long working days and nights, all that money saved, still all we had to show for it was a crippled catastrophe. More work, more work, endless work. I just wanted to rest. I was so weary, so tired, so burned out, and so afraid—always feeling afraid, inadequate, unworthy. And so I refused to continue. I would not, and could not.

"I'm going for a walk," I announced defiantly as soon as we pulled in. I expected a fight.

"Whatever," he said with resignation.

God! I'd done it! I didn't have to stay and toil, forcing myself to perform a thousand little inane tasks just to please him, the more mindless the better so I didn't have to feel anything. *Amazing!* I grabbed a small sandwich bag of homemade applesauce-raisin cookies made from Amanda apples, and walked away. I was leaving, running, looking for space, looking for freedom from a demon and a set of circumstances I couldn't even name.

I headed up the road beyond our house. The day was cool, wet, and grey. My work boots swung rhythmically out in front of me, gulping bites of road, sand and pebbles grinding beneath my heels. With each determined stride my long brown braid swung back and forth like the pendulum of a grandfather clock, counting, measuring, keeping track of this borrowed time, perhaps. My hands had burrowed into my sweatshirt pockets, my left one nestling the bag of cookies. No doubt unconsciously I had jutted out my chin, crimping the back of my neck. That was my walk, the one I had gotten teased about in college.

Presently, the road hugged the western side of this high, narrow valley. Down to my left was the neighbors' house.

The epitome of any home builder's dream, it sat, artificially raised above the valley floodplain by a mound of gravel, neat, new, complete, warm, functional. Envy, jealousy, and angst arose within. Why did a life like that always seem to belong to someone else? No matter. I was walking now.

The scent of balsam fir brought my head around to my right. A thick border of the stunted dark green trees clung to the small road cut at the bottom of a steep slope. In my mind I saw a magnificent yellow birch ("curly birch" was the colloquial name for these tawny-barked trees adorned with ringlets of papery gold) my husband and I had found up on that hill when we first surveyed the land. What a tree, really big, the biggest of its kind I'd ever seen. I remembered that as the two of us discussed the probable quality of the lumber, I had felt disjointed inside. To be thinking of, let alone articulating, the callous dissection and utilization of such a presence resonated with a very old and deep pain inside of me, vestiges of the double life I seemed to live so well. Why couldn't I have defended the tree? What persistent muzzle prevented the formation of the truth upon my tongue? Not that it was ours to cut. The land upon which it reigned was part of a 15-acre parcel adjoining our property which had not been included in the sale. I didn't wonder that I had never been able to find that tree again.

The road ended as such and became a private drive. No longer maintained by the town, the uniformly taupe gravel surface now stretched into two brown grooves bordering a grassy tuft. Not too high above my head crisscrossing white pine boughs wove a long green arching tent, and to either side their narrow black trunks shimmered in and out of manmade square and diagonal patterns against a soft, rusty needle mat. As I walked, this stretch of road became a transition between cultivation and its absence. I anticipated the wild with excitement, at the same time I left civilization with fear.

The road opened briefly from the regular cover of white pine and descended, curving to the left as it crossed the creek. I stopped on the bridge in the deafening sound of the rushing water. I felt the rhythms reverberating through me, resonating peace. I beheld the banks of the creek, crowded with ferns and mosses, looking like a magic world in miniature, complete, simple, a place of wee folk, pixies, fairies, and devas.

I turned and walked again, soon passing the last of the seasonal camps. The road rose gently, eroded further and further into an alternately muddy and rocky trail. I crisscrossed the stream several different times, and walked and walked … breathing deeply the alternately sweet and musky air, thinking of everything and nothing at the same time. I crossed the stream one more time—it was now on my left. The road climbed suddenly, arcing around to the left. At first, the stream remained far below, until by means of a series of irregular stone steps and falls it began to gain elevation and catch up.

A quiet surface of shimmering light far below caught my eye. Sitting at the base of a four-foot mossy ledge was a modest pool. Several crystal strands of water braided their way down the dark green-lipped schists, entering the bowl.

The onslaught of time stood still here, and for a moment so did I. But something hard in me pushed forward, resisting the softness of this place. I walked on, climbing higher and higher, thinking I'd find something better, bigger, prettier. But my inner drive was dissipating. The further I got from that place, the more I wanted to go back. Finally, I stopped, debating. Something I wasn't sure I wanted to feel was calling to me. Finally, I gave in. I turned and retraced my steps. Back to the water.

The pool looked different from this direction, smaller, simpler, and not quite so magnificent. I doubted my desire to return. But there I was. I stepped over the edge of the road cut, slipping and scrambling down the steep bank, leaving dark earthen skid marks behind me, churning up dank earthen smells. Down at the water's edge, I found the pool to be more magical than ever, with a mere trickle of sound. I walked out on a coarse, sandy crescent that formed its downstream barrier. My boots sank and as I saw water rushing in to surround them I jumped back. I imagined how bracing the cold sediment would feel pressing against my bare heels and arches, squeezing between my toes. I stepped further back to sit on a rock and removed my boots and socks. Then I stood.

The gentle gurgle of water beckoned. I bent over to roll up my pant legs to mid-calf and stepped out once again, working my feet around in the scratchy stuff, venturing right up to the water's edge. There I stopped. My feet were freezing, but I wanted to go in all the way even as a dull aching flame engulfed my ankles and licked at my shins. But something stopped me: thoughts of being seen, of being caught, yes, but more than that. It was as if there was an invisible wall between me and the perfection of this place. It was as if I had not been invited to come in.

A recently read book on Native American teachings helped shape my humility into action. I thought of the bag of cookies in my pocket and reached in to pull them out. They were squished and crumbly. Carrying the bag in one hand I groped my way, three-legged, along the rocks toward The Great Mossy Ledge, which felt to me like an altar or shrine. I balanced myself precariously and offered up a crumbled cookie, or maybe all the cookies, with a slight apology for their humble state. I felt compelled to remind the spirit(s) of the pool that the cookies were homemade with love and totally natural. Gripping a small wet outcropping with my left hand, I reached as high as I could and lovingly snugged several offerings in various nooks and crannies. Then I tucked the empty bag into my pocket and withdrew, moving more easily now with four available gropers.

This time when I walked out onto the sand-spit the invisible wall was gone. The resistance had melted away both inside and out. Rejoicing yet cautious and alert, I removed my clothes, placing each item carefully on a rock nearby, one on top of the other. Then, step by step, I descended into the pool's maybe three-foot crystal depths. The chill was exciting and exhilarating. It was also almost unbearable. But I did bare myself to it wholly and completely. I dunked in maybe three times, crouching down and springing up, crouching down and springing up, crouching down and springing up.

I was unbelievably happy.

I was also unbelievably cold. I rushed out of the water and with numb fingers I reached for and donned each article of clothing in what felt like an interminable ritual. Too soon, though, I was dressed. A hot stinging chill electrified my skin against the cloth. The wall had not returned, but already I felt a sadness of separation. I withdrew to the rock and sat back to put on my socks and boots. I'm not sure why it made sense to wipe and dry my whitened feet with my socks and then put them on, but it did. Then I stood, strangely warm. Of course I said "Thank you" and "Good-bye." It was just my way.

Hand over hand and feet, I climbed the embankment, wishing I had been more careful not to leave such scars coming down. Up and over, and I was back on the road heading home. My braid, heavy and wet, stayed in the middle of my back now, soaking through my sweatshirt and turtleneck, pressing a single cold line against my skin. A steady stream of droplets formed and fell from the pigtail end, soaking through the back of my pants.

I felt free and strong and alive and so much more than fine.

CHAPTER THIRTEEN

Snowy Owl

"Superhuman qualities and near-human appearance of the owl—its upright perch, mortal stare, fantastic vision, and nightly screams—especially evoked mystery and awe. History as well as iconography connects the owl with important goddesses such as Athena, the Greek goddess of knowledge and wisdom...."

—Marija Gimbutas, *The Living Goddesses*

SPRING, 1990

IT WAS MAY AND my spirits were high. I was re-applying to college at the University of Vermont, and would start with summer term in a month. Soon, I would be immersed in field courses that would have me traveling all over the Champlain Valley: to understand glaciation by examining sand-dunes halfway up surrounding ridges; or geological inversions where ancient bedrock had been exposed resting on top of much newer formations; or digging deep holes to examine soil horizons; or spelunking limestone caves to learn about erosion by following underground streams; or hiking up to the Madison hut for an overnight, in order to hike out through the Great Gulf Wilderness the following day. Among many new and fascinating aspects of natural history, I would learn that the schist bedrock of the Green Mountains, entirely distinct from that of the Adirondacks or the White Mountains, imparts a sweetness and richness to the soil and hence the vegetation, an insight that would cause me to reflect on the many sweet adventures I had been having there. But in that moment on that particular morning I knew only that I was re-inventing my life. I would move out of my parents' house, leave my marriage behind, and go forth to new horizons.

It was a beautifully clear blue morning with brilliant sun. Inspired to take a long walk, I had my sister with whom I had spent the night drop me off at a dirt road up on the ridge about five miles from my parents' house. I had in mind a back way that would eventually get me to the road descending the hill behind their house. I was pretty sure I knew the way from cross-country skiing even if I had never walked the exact route before.

To match my lighthearted mood the thawing roadway was firm but springy under my Birkenstocks. I almost felt like skipping. The sun was hot on my face, head, and shoulders, and I welcomed every ray. What a bucolic paradise surrounded me and how lucky I felt to be alive on this day! Like the vistas before me, possibilities for a better and more satisfying life were opening up. I was only thirty-one. Not too late to realize latent dreams.

After about fifteen minutes, I came to an expected four-corners intersection with dairy farms all around and took a left onto a different road. I followed this due north until I spied a familiar right fork onto a lesser road which eventually became a path through woods. At this point it started to descend and as I descended with it I encountered granular spring corn-snow underfoot. Only a thin covering at first, but soon enough it was four inches, six inches, eight, ten, twelve, until I was struggling to take each step in heavy wet snow, still descending and not knowing how much farther or how much deeper it would go.

The Birkenstocks that had at first proved a wonderful way to celebrate spring weather after eight months of heavy winter boots couldn't have been less appropriate for this descent back through the seasons. Not only were they open sandals, but the crisp cork edges kept catching on the snow, and on a couple of occasions I wasn't sure how my foot would ever come free. I was definitely not skipping now. Each step was a major feat of engineering, twisting, turning, tugging, wiggling, and no one like the last. Onward I pressed, much preferring this direct shortcut through woods to having to go back out and around on roads I didn't know very well, not to mention very likely doubling the distance. I would have to make it through. *Geez, I hoped I would make it through!* Luckily, the thick wool of my now soaking wet socks held the cold somewhat at bay.

Finally, I came to the bottom of what was a deep ravine, wrestling each foot through about about eighteen inches of snow. As I struggled on the other side to ascend, I looked up at one point and not twenty feet from me perched on a tree stump was a large snowy owl. She looked directly at me with her probing eyes. I stopped my struggling, and looked directly at her. I'd never seen such a creature, but the owl-ness of the upright posture, elongated body, pure white coloration, and arresting eyes allowed only one possibility, although apparition, guardian, angel, or ghost would all have been reasonable alternate presumptions. There was intensity and electricity in the air between us.

After a breathless moment, an unrecognizable sound pulled my head around briefly in the other direction. When I looked back, the owl was gone. Without making a sound, she had simply disappeared. I looked all around, still hoping to catch a glimpse, but there was no other movement or trace. At the time, I didn't know anything about snowy owls, certainly not about their ability to move in silence, so for a long time, I wondered if what I had witnessed was an impossibility. I also didn't know snowy owls are native to arctic regions and so to stumble across one in the backwoods of Vermont was a rare event, indeed. Or that, unlike most owls, they're comfortable hunting both day and night and are known for their uncanny knack for being in the right place at the right time to acquire food with a minimum of effort, unlike most birds of prey, by waiting for nourishment to come to them.

I did, however, sense that something extraordinary had taken place. As I ascended up and out of the ravine, the snow depth eventually diminishing back down to nothing and each step easier than the last, I mused that somehow in the midst of my clumsy, clunking clamber through the woods, I had been graced again with something altogether sublime. Though many years, many struggles, and many ravines still lay ahead, what I would only much later come to understand about my journey in this lifetime is that deep spiritual nourishment would find me again and again in these serendipitous moments being in nature, walking on the Earth. Against the pressure of a doing, achieving, accomplishing society, I would ultimately find communion by just being, and allowing the gifts of depth, insight, and freedom to come to me.

CHAPTER FOURTEEN

The Crash

"In the face of setbacks and delays, ask yourself:
What is this preparing me for?"

—Claire Zammit, *Feminine Power*

1993

I'LL NEVER FORGET MY first, and most dramatic, energy crash. I had just completed my undergraduate degree, Magna Cum Laude. My divorce had now been final for a couple of years, and I had also recently ended another relationship—one which had taken me out to Colorado with my partner and his three young children—but ultimately returning to Vermont on my own. I had just finished watching the entire four hours of the feature film, "Gettysburg," in a sparsely attended theatre one weekday afternoon. When the lights came up, I couldn't move. Somehow my legs would not obey my inclination to rise from my seat. My chest felt heavy, my head foggy, dizzy even. But I was alone. I had driven myself to the theatre and there was only me to get myself home. *What to do? Is it blood sugar?* I had been diagnosed with low blood sugar several years before, but had managed to keep it under control with plenty of protein at meals and as snacks in between. Okay, so maybe I needed protein. I'd go to the nearest restaurant I could find in South Burlington, and get a burger. Surely something that hearty would make me feel better.

With that thought, I managed to get up out of my seat and drag myself to my car, all the while hoping I could even drive safely. I made my way by taking everything in small bite-sized chunks, narrating out loud to keep myself focused: *Unlock car. Get in. Close door. Fasten seat belt. Insert key and turn. Okay, driving now. Turn signal. Watch traffic. Watch the lights. Careful.* Later, having found a restaurant, ordered and eaten a burger exactly as planned, the result was that only marginal equilibrium had been restored. If only I could get home, I would surely feel better after a good night's sleep. Yes, perhaps I had run myself down. With this beacon of hope, I made my way slowly back to my rented room and into bed.

I awoke the next morning, feeling somewhere betwixt and between. I was scheduled for a catering event that night as waitstaff. The money was good. The trays would be heavy. The pace fast. I rested all day in anticipation. I showed up and worked for about an hour. But then I nearly passed out and asked to sit down. After 15 minutes, I asked to be sent home. The next day I scheduled an appointment with a homeopath. I didn't know much about homeopathy but being cut from alternative cloth, I thought perhaps I would find a magical cure. From the symptoms and dark circles under my eyes, he diagnosed me with adrenal exhaustion and prescribed some white powder—to be taken three times a day. How long before I would feel better? Three months was his prediction.

I went home and called my parents. Would they support me for a few months? I didn't want to leave my room in this shared house. I wanted to stay and get back on my feet. Yes, they would support me. But only if I agreed to see a "real" doctor. Okay. I picked a name out of the phone book and made the appointment. The upshot of his examination a week or so later was essentially the same: chronic fatigue syndrome, although he suspected the underlying cause to be candidiasis. "Western medicine doesn't recognize this diagnosis, and the test for it is inconclusive and expensive," he said. "Instead, read this book, Candidiasis, and follow the recommendations." From the book I learned that out of over 200 possible symptoms I had about three-quarters of them—everything from the dramatic onset of extreme fatigue, to weight loss, to chronic digestive issues, a bloated belly, to excruciating fibromyalgia in my shoulders, heart palpitations, a knocking in my ears, and strange patches of leathery skin on my elbows, feet, and toes.

The regime was a strict diet—with no starches or sugars, no yeast, no fermented foods, no fungi or possible mold; no tea of any kind, or salt or pepper or spices. Lots of fat-free yogurt, but no cheese, no butter; only organic low-fat meats (poultry and fish) and low-starch vegetables; no potatoes or fruit. No grains. Lots of supplements in a complex array, depending upon the number of times taken per day, with food, without food, etc. Oh, and just for kicks, an antidepressant from the doctor, who remarked, "Who wouldn't be depressed with all your symptoms? And if you get discouraged about how long it takes you to get well, just remember how long it took you to get this sick." (Thirty-some years?) Small comfort.

I was supposed to be launching my life! I had finally graduated from college. I had been accepted to graduate school but deferred to take a detour, to try something rather bohemian for a year—to dance! Anyway, it didn't matter now. Now I could barely climb stairs. My days would include: getting up, eating a large breakfast of yogurt and poached eggs (exhausting), and dragging myself back up to my room (exhausting) to lie down, to listen to guided meditations, to pray for all I was worth, maybe to read a little (exhausting) … until one day a recollection came to me of a most unusual experience I had had one afternoon a few years before on a wintry hillside. Perhaps I would just try to recount that one spectacularly mysterious and almost inexplicable event. As soon as I started to type it up, not only did it present itself to me in great detail, but a whole array of other such stories came to mind, long forgotten, but somehow there, waiting patiently all that time. Over a series of writing sessions, they now poured forth through my tapping fingers and onto my computer screen. I did not see myself as a writer. They sort of seemed to write themselves. And so, in a pattern of breakfast, writing, resting, lunch, napping, dinner, bed, I endured that first fragile month of what would ultimately become an unpredictable lifetime journey of recovery. And the stories that poured out of me so unexpectedly would define the earthly journey of awakening that has subtly guided and shaped the rest of my life.

CHAPTER FIFTEEN

Divinely Feminine

"The connection between moisture, life, and the life-giving goddesses contained deep cosmological significance. Human life began in the watery realm of a woman's womb. So, by analogy, the goddess was the source of all human, plant, and animal life. She ruled all water sources: lakes, rivers, springs, wells, and rain clouds."

—Marija Gimbutas, *The Living Goddesses*

AUGUST, 1996

ON A GREY HAZY day, I had just returned from a walk on the beach with my parents and found myself in the midst of an unexpected encounter. My parents recognized a couple—the son and daughter-in-law of the man who had been headmaster of the school when my parents were interns so many years before, and who had introduced them to this beautiful harbor. As they approached the couple, I held back. Although I had just managed to complete my Masters in Elementary Education earlier that year, I had also relapsed into chronic fatigue in the midst of my search for a teaching position and had withdrawn all of my job applications. Feelings ashamed and uncertain about myself and my future, I was barely listening to the conversation, focused instead on gathering my belongings in anticipation of our departure. Until, that is, my father said very pointedly, "That sounds like something Katy would be interested in!"

All eyes turned to me. "Excuse me, what was that?" I asked, looking up, embarrassed. And so the daughter-in-law described to me a nine-month program in Women's Spirituality she was offering. Coincidentally, it would start in one month, in Cambridge, MA, one town over from Arlington, where I was scheduled soon to move to live near my new boyfriend whom I had met in graduate school. While the details of her description remained a bit of a blur, I politely agreed that it sounded very interesting, and she said, "Great! We still have spaces available. I'll send you a brochure."

When the brochure arrived, and I actually looked it over, the richness and mystery of the course description moved me deeply. Coincidentally, one of the two other teachers was also connected to the same coastal village, and had long been revered in our family for her beautiful pottery. Her lamps and pie plates had been exchanged as gifts as I was growing up, although she had since transitioned to a career in Jungian Analysis and no longer labored with clay. Looking back, I would describe what transpired in the next couple of weeks as divinely guided: I searched for and found a manageable part-time education-related job and an affordable place to live; I successfully arranged to defer payments on my student loans; and my parents offered to gift me with the fee for entry into the program. Dumbfounded, and grateful, I accepted.

And so, a month later, with the after school program job under way which I secretly prayed my limited strength and marginal health could sustain, and having moved into an inexpensive room in a group house I hoped I could afford, I showed up for the first Friday evening session of the program's first weekend retreat. After registering, I walked into a long room with soft lighting. About 25 women were seated upon cushions set in an oblong circle around a centerpiece of elegantly draped cloth, candles, and various figurines. Most of the spaces were filled, but a cushion directly in front of me was not, so I quickly sat down, curious to see whatever was about to take place.

With the simple ringing of a chime, we came to silent attention. In her resonant, gently compelling voice, the daughter-in-law I had met so fortuitously invited us to arrive—by closing our eyes, taking several deep breaths in and out, by settling into our bodies, by feeling the weight of our hips on the pillows, on the floor, on Mother Earth. When she invited us to open our eyes, she explained the overall structure of the program: one weekend intensive a month, followed by weekly Tuesday evening integration sessions. All three leaders were psychotherapists and artists. Each introduced herself, and each participant was likewise invited to introduce herself. I remember little of what I or anyone said. What none of us could yet envision was that getting to know ourselves and each other in the wake of this life-changing work would continue many years past the conclusion of the programmed nine months.

Introductions that evening were followed by a slideshow of the work of Marija Gimbutas, a Lithuanian-born archeologist, recently deceased, who, after gaining world renown as an expert in the burial mounds of Iron Age Europe, found her authority and reputation alienated from mainstream academia when she undertook to catalogue, study, and introduce theories about what she kept finding in the layer just underneath those burial mounds: goddess figurines. Her excavations indicated a widespread array of communities, each with as many as ten thousand inhabitants, persisting from about 10,000 to 3,000 B.C.E. in what Dr. Gimbutas coined as Old Europe. From a meticulous and ground-breaking multidisciplinary cross referencing of ancient artifacts and modern linguistic and folkloric evidence, she was able to describe this culture in great detail.

I was riveted by the world she conjured:

Peaceful - lacking weapons or defenses of any kind. *What?! Having been raised in the ongoing tragedy, tension, and anxiety of World Wars I and II, "the Bomb," the Cold War, Detente, ICBMs and the ever-present threat of nuclear annihilation, how could I even begin to take this in?*

Stable - persisting for thousands of years. *What?! How could so many civilizations so widespread thrive without inner and outer conflict? What about all those supposed club-wielding "cavemen" and the characterization of "Man" as naturally violent?*

Egalitarian - *What?! No dwellings bigger than others, and all ancestral remains treated equally? No "haves" and "have-nots"? All sharing in the wealth and abundance?*

Matrifocal/matrilineal - *What?! Honoring women and tracing lineage through the mother line? Carry my grandmother's grandmother's grandmother's name? Not so that men have always and "naturally" dominated women? Patriarchy itself only five thousand years old—not always and not forever?*

Earth and goddess worshipping - *What?! A plethora of ovens, urns, bowls and figurines expertly crafted and artfully designed, and an alphabet older than any other script known, all expressing the divinity of the Feminine archetype and Mother Earth? No angry God towering over and instilling fear, shame, and submission?*

Dr. Gimbutas went on to trace a series of repeated incursions over several thousand years by hierarchical, patriarchal warrior tribes who worshipped a punishing sky-god, overthrowing these cultures and dispersing them to the farthest reaches of their last strongholds—Minoan Crete, Ireland, Lithuania. She predicted that it would take the academic community 35 years to fully appreciate her work—and indeed subsequent research has consistently upheld her findings.

I stared in open-mouthed wonder at the slides, introduced slowly enough that we could let them speak to us, so that we could feel their impact. The wellspring of possibilities for peace and prosperity presented by ancient images of a woman-honoring world began to lift the burden of internalized misogyny, and offered a renewed sense of purpose for us as women to embody the re-awakening of Divine Feminine potential in the context of our painfully patriarchal world. And together over the next nine months, through discussion, sharing, ritual, dance, art, writing, reading, and study, we absorbed and integrated profound new understandings, healed deep wounds, and learned to express the inexpressible.

What a strange juxtaposition this presented for me: to be embodied when my health was so fragile, to go out evenings when my energy was so low, to attend potlucks when my menu options were so narrow and unvarying. To be forced to lie across my cushion on the floor when my stomach hurt so badly I could hardly breathe. The immersion was both calming and stirring, reassuring and upsetting, soothing and tumultuous. The story of the overthrow of Old European cultures—of patriarchal, hierarchical, warlike, nomadic tribes overthrowing and erasing these beautifully undefended matrifocal settlements—was my story, our story. In these last 5,000 years of patriarchy, how had each of us ourselves been erased, been overthrown and silenced, our natural inclinations rebuffed, our extraordinary gifts and unique contributions dismissed, by the misogyny of Western European culture?

For me personally, who had hated the powerlessness I had grown up with of being "just a girl," suffering such anxiety under the most extreme and insane expressions of patriarchal power-over mentality possible, the reverberations of Marija's findings were tectonic. For the first time in my life, as an Earth-loving woman I felt connected to something so ancient, so subterranean, so profound, so beautiful, that it filled me with power and offered a sense of identity and voice: *Divine Feminine. Spiritual Feminist.*

I was starting to know who I was.

I was unable to share these deep awakenings with my new boyfriend. The first few times I tried to talk about them, we ended up in a fight. He accused me of being shallow and naive. He read one of the books I had read, and castigated it as having been poorly written, and lacking any real, substantial argument. Couldn't I see that? Was I so incapable of sophisticated intellectual discernment?

If I had had any shred of self-respect, I'd have ended our relationship right then and there. But instead, it took a troubled marriage and almost another twenty years for me to recognize the irony of my predicament: a 21st-century equivalent of the peaceable Earth-loving goddess worshipper subjugated and oppressed by the ruthless, conquering warrior.

During the nine months of the Women's Spirituality program, what I couldn't eat *actually*, I consumed *spiritually*. I practiced ritual, sang goddess chants, explored hands-on healing, learned to play an African djembe from an African American goddess whose mission was to empower women by putting a drum between their legs (I know, right?), and fell deeply in love with the power of gathering in sacred space reverently, intentionally and spiritually with women. When the program ended, I felt pregnant with something I couldn't name. Full to bursting. While on summer vacation from my after-school job, I rekindled a long-abandoned dream to nurture my artistic inclinations: by systematically working my way through the 12-week program offered in *The Artist's Way*, by Julia Cameron. Out of that poured a story I turned into a one-woman show which I performed in about 25 venues over the next several years, and an accompanying hand-crafted booklet illustrated with my own pen and ink renderings of ancient pre-historic Old European art. And over the course of that first unlikely year of ritual storytelling performance art my energy returned. I emerged miraculously out of chronic fatigue. My stomach settled and I dared once again to eat whatever I wished. Unbelievably, I would go on to lead an active life, hiking mountains, riding my bike, and launching my intended career as an elementary educator.

AUGUST, 2001

I WAS AT THE family camp in northern Ontario, Canada, with my parents, my eldest sister, my brother, his wife, daughter, and teenage step-daughter who had brought a friend. We were visiting during a terrible drought. Day after day of hot, dry, heavy windless air. The typically bracing lake water became tepid and covered with a thin layer of what looked like scum. Pollen, maybe? The island, little more than rocks covered in pine needles, crackled and crunched underfoot.

I was glad to be there but struggling to be at ease with various tensions within the extended family. Toward the end of our stay, everyone but my parents went on a three-day camping trip up the lake to a beloved inlet known from childhood, with clear, turquoise water. On the first night, we were cooking dinner over a campfire, when a helicopter flew overhead. That had never happened before. Shortly thereafter, a couple of canoes approached us and the occupants called out to say that there was an open-fire ban due to the drought. We were terribly embarrassed not to have known, and to have caused such concern. We were also dismayed that unless we found a camp stove to borrow, we would be eating peanut butter sandwiches for the remainder of our trip.

The next day, having tried and failed to source such a stove, we paddled a ways up the inlet to have a picnic lunch. Seemed innocent enough, but a ferocious head-wind blew up on our way back. We paddled for all we were worth, making only inches with each stroke. It amazed me that we could make any progress at all in a wind like that, a testament to the genius of the canoe itself, and to our determination and strength as the paddlers we were raised to be. The next day, when we decided to break camp early and paddle home, my shoulders were tired and sore. It was all I could do to take each stroke.

Our departure was only days away, and I was seeking to regain my psychic center which had been thrown off by two weeks amidst this awkward family gathering, the drought, the exhaustion that followed our desperate paddle against the wind, and the inner turbulence all this had inspired. I was so sad for the land, for this childhood lake that I loved, a deeply embedded and formative part of my identity. I pondered the imbalances that the drought represented: global climate change, the relentless hunger of corporate industrialization at the apex of the last five thousand years of patriarchy, of power-over culture, men over women, head over heart, humans over nature. What could I do to nourish this deeply desiccated world?

I held this question like a prayer, not knowing and feeling at a loss. And then, on the last full day before we were to depart the island, I began menstruating. In a flash of insight, I received this as the answer to my query: I was inspired to try offering my moon blood back to the Earth as symbolic nourishment for the parched land. Among many forays into indigenous and Earth-worshipping culture and lore, I had read about women doing this back since the beginning of time, as a way of honoring the bounty of Mother Earth.

I had never actually offered my moon blood to the Earth, but decided that amidst busy preparations for our departure, I would take a moment to be alone. With the lower half of me wrapped only in a towel I found a secluded place overlooking the lake and lowered myself onto the pine-needly ground. In truth, it was tricky and prickly, but in my heart and soul there were greater things at stake.

Eyes closed, I sat in quiet contemplation and prayer for I knew not how long, trying to connect psychically to the countless generations of women through time so similarly called. If the Divine Feminine was to reawaken in the

21st century to heal the planet, it would have to happen through each and every one of us. I tried to envision the world of peace and abundance as I would have it be, to embody my power as co-creator of my own reality. Out of this deep, doubting, reverie I began to hear a faint pitter-patter around me and felt something land on my nose. I opened my eyes to see that I was momentarily overshadowed by a tiny cloud, with the lightest little rain falling only in my immediate vicinity. In wild disbelief, I waited quietly and watched it pass in a short minute or two. I knew the amount of actual rainfall was insignificant, and that it was likely not witnessed or experienced by anyone but me. And how then would I ever begin to explain?

I have never before attempted to tell this tale, but I swear it is true. In the moment, I wondered dreamily at the resilience and readiness of the nature-spirits-natural-world-divine-mirror to communicate so directly! As if she/they wanted me to know that my honest and heartfelt effort, unschooled and inadequate as it may have been, had not gone unnoticed or unappreciated. Imagine the untapped potential of such a magical and co-creative reality, the one our Western-rational-objective-scientific paradigm has been telling us doesn't exist! Imagine the world we could enjoy in this kind of sacred interrelationship.

EPIPHANY:

Dancing with the Divine

"And without this bonding, this joining of two living beings, what is life? What is life without this exchange of soul essence...?"

—Stephen Harrod Buhner, *The Secret Teachings of Plants*

I HAVE COME A long way from the young child who thought her life might virtually be over if she did not find that storage closet key—who prayed for her salvation out of desperation, and was rewarded by finding it under a pile of decomposing leaves—*in nature.* How did I know to do that? Perhaps my limited five-year-old consciousness was simply programmed to survive at all costs and was prepared to try anything, even if it meant reaching out beyond probabilities to virtual impossibilities.

I did not know then that I was a spiritual being having a human experience. Nature taught me that. Nature came calling again and again while I was busy trying, however imperfectly, to craft a very human life. *Earthly Nature* guided me to my *Eternal Nature*—unbounded by the confines of everyday experience. An eternity which reaches through the fabric of time and space to whisper brilliant, poetic mysteries and unlimited potentialities, unearthing questions of meaning and purpose, such as, *Why am I here?*

Many years of not knowing the answer to this question have led me to this moment and this page. The providential course on Folklore and the Supernatural at the university so long ago had inspired a desire to overcome psychic limitations of the rational, objective worldview of Western culture within which I found myself. While living a life bounded by material limits, I sensed greater meaning and possibilities just beyond reach.

For lack of skill or deeper understanding, a dichotomy between the ordinary and the extraordinary continued well into middle age as I struggled to integrate outer worldly endeavors with rich inner glimpses of the unknown. These unexpected encounters in nature gained momentum over time, gradually evolving into deliberate explorations with books, big ideas, and a stimulating variety of experiential programs. At some point I started referring to them as mystical awakenings, although it would still be a while before I understood, awakening to what?

And so this is my story of salvation. How extraordinary circumstances in the backwoods of Vermont presented themselves again and again to mirror something back to me that for many years I was not yet ready to see: my divinity. If I grew up with any notions of God they would have been more akin to an angry, guilt-inducing, overbearing menace. Certainly I had no conception of the Divine as a sudden unfocused inclination, a whimsical encounter, a gentle caress of sun-speckled water, a summons to lunar wildness, a quiet moment of stillness and communion. Nor, certainly, as dancing footprints winding and weaving over a wintry hillside, turkeys on a wild trot, a playful and mischievous young beaver, magic apples of gratitude and grace, tree-beings offering salutations, an owl's prescient blessing in a deep ravine.

And what was it about water and its repeated summoning of me to engage, to immerse, to cast conventions to the wind and plunge gasping into it? Water counterbalanced the earth-fire furnace of my becoming: cooling, cleansing, purifying and soothing, offering relief from chronic stomach pain and other somatic symptoms; allowing me to express my free spirit, so often weighted down and heavy in the flesh and blood of daily life. While my spirit always wanted to dance, to flow like liquid gold, my body often felt so leaden, so encumbered. Water was playful and freeing; liberating me from gravity's pull, allowing my body to dance and twirl and to do somersaults, handstands, and handsprings long past when I could do them on dry land. Immersed in water, I could act *as if*. Water was shocking, and energizing. *Water is awakening!*

Water for me has always been a touchstone of possibility. In 2000, I went on a tour of the Black Madonna in France, where I was deeply moved to learn that even the grandest cathedrals are built on top of ancient holy wells. Even when I was in the throes of adrenal exhaustion and chronic fatigue, when I didn't have the energy to swim, I could still float on the water's surface. And in the inner silence of water-filled ears, I could attune to the rhythm of my own breath, and let myself be gently supported and rocked.

For my fiftieth birthday, I took myself to see that persecuted and now world renowned spiritual healer in Brazil known as John of God whom I had read about in college. Although greatly relieved to discover that I could choose not to have him stick a rusty knife into my eye sockets, I experienced powerful healing; I was significantly if subtly altered by the experience. A year later, I quit an unhappy job to join a seven-month apprenticeship in nature-based spiritual and energetic healing in, you got it: Vermont. The teachings immediately gave voice to lifelong musings: about the nature of reality; the spirit and sentience of nature; and alternate approaches to significant transformations for ourselves, each other, and the Earth. Unlike in my folklore class, I did not develop a crush on the teacher of this course. But deep admiration and appreciation for her grew. I basked in the glow of her vibrant energy, deep commitment, extensive knowledge, and iconoclastic spirit. As with the folklore class, my head and heart wanted to explode. My whole being rang like a bell, as if all the labyrinthine twists and turns in my life had been preparing me for this.

Modern humans around the globe, I was told, suffer from homesickness in being separated from nature. And I was one of the lucky ones to be finding my way home. Drawing from both ancient indigenous wisdom and ground-breaking science, we learned that our bodies are instruments of resonance, carefully refined over millions of evolutionary years to be in perfect harmony with nature in general, and plants—Green Beings—in particular. We learned that plants have spiritual presence and are eager to share their unique healing gifts with us. All we have to do is tune in and allow profound connections to be made.

This is our birthright. And our responsibility as humans is to be in a co-creative partnership with the world around us—with all that is.

Over the next seven months, I spent hours and hours sitting with Green Beings. Through sight, touch, smell, taste, and sound, I invited their spiritual energies to infuse my senses and wake me up. Bonding with these "healing allies" wildly affirmed my lifetime of mysterious wanderings.

At long last, a brittle shell of confusion and doubt cracked open and a new reality was born:

No separation. All Is One. Where nature's myriad forms whisper a poetic language of meaning and purpose and intention. Where nature is interactive and responsive, seeking to engage in a divine dance of co-creation when we allow her to do so. When we let her in. And when we pay attention, we can be the key to unlocking mysteries beyond imagining.

Backyard Labyrinth

"In the labyrinth, everything is connected; the beginning is also the end ...this experience of oneness has been referred to by mystics of all traditions as the goal of life: to realize the truth of unity."

—Bailey Cunningham, *Mandala: Journey to the Center*

I CURRENTLY LIVE IN an unremarkable neighborhood in a small unremarkable 1950s cape on an equally unimpressive quarter-acre plot of land. My home is within walking distance of two public wooded parks and the downtown area of a city of less than 25,000. My postage stamp of a front yard places me closer than I would like to a street that can be busy, noisy, and dusty. My very long and narrow property spans two streets, and is lined on three sides by tall sugar maples. To many people, there is nothing very special about this place.

But this land speaks to me, and has for many years. It spoke to me first on an ordinary September afternoon when I was out raking leaves about a year after I'd moved here with my second husband. With golden light from a retiring sun alighting on tree trunks and the surrounding leafy duff, and with the pleasant musty scent of decomposition teasing my nostrils, I was suddenly filled with a familiar sense of wonder and awe. Time and space expanded within me and around me as I stopped and leaned on my rake to more deeply experience the moment. My heart bloomed with inexplicable joy.

This was not otherwise a time of much joy in my life. My husband and I had recently moved to this community for his work, after many years of anticipation. During those years, I had consoled myself that our difficult marriage and my own sense of meaning and purpose were all going to come together once we had made the move. Instead, I felt lost, lonely, abandoned and alienated, anxious about everything—work, money, the marriage, and myself. Despite repeated blessings of synchronicity and grace, my waking consciousness continued to identify as downtrodden and put-upon, sadly dissevered from the truth of my own divinity.

Mystical moments in nature stood in direct contrast to this grind of daily life. In them, I was free of mind, light of heart, expressive of body—immersed in beauty, enveloped in grace. And here, again, in this moment mystical bliss was welling up from the ground under my feet! Memories of other such magical moments flooded in, but the fact that I was merely standing in my own small, unremarkable backyard set this moment apart. *What can this possibly be about?* I could only remain curious to see whether more might be revealed.

And revealed it was. It came to me first the following summer as an impulse to reinvent the awkward layout of the backyard. I began by chopping down a wall of shrubs that had been cutting the yard in half, and by removing an unsightly chicken-wire fence. Suddenly, the yard became whole, though still long and narrow and mostly shaded, not lending itself easily to visions of elegant landscaping. But whole.

Months later, in the depths of winter, it came to me in a flash of insight that in the very back area of the yard that had only recently come into view I would create a labyrinth! Unlike mazes, labyrinths are designed with a single winding path into the center and back out again. Though still mostly shrouded in mystery, they are thought to be spiritual mechanisms of healing, rebalancing, and divination. One can ask a question upon entering and find the answer as a result of walking slowly with intention, twisting and turning all the way in and all the way out. Creating a labyrinth would accomplish two things: honor my growing connection with this land, and establish a sacred intent for it.

I didn't know what kind of labyrinth. I didn't know how big or how fashioned. So, I ordered a book on labyrinths, resolved to let the land decide.

In the summer of 2007, pendulum in hand, I walked out back to hold an intentional conversation with the land. I had been working with a pendulum as an energetic healing technique with myself and other people for only a couple of years but had never before tried working with it in this way. To use my pendulum as a guide, I went out to the back area in question and held the pendulum in front of me. First I asked permission to undertake this inquiry on behalf of the land and watched the pendulum swing enthusiastically in a clockwise direction, signaling *Yes*. Then I asked, "Do you want a labyrinth here?" *Yes*. "Where is the center of this labyrinth?" And walked around while continuing to hold the pendulum out in front of me until I got another *Yes* and marked the spot with a stone. "Where is the perimeter of this labyrinth?" I walked outward from the center until I got another *Yes* and marked it with another stone. "How many rings will this labyrinth have—One? Two? Three? Four? Five? Six? Seven?" *Yes*. "Seven. Okay."

To determine how wide each of the seven rings would be, I got a tape measure and extended it from the stone marking the center to the stone marking the perimeter, only to find that it measured exactly 21 feet. Confirmation that greater powers were clearly at work filled me with a familiar wave of expansiveness. Not only was the measurement exact, but seven divided so perfectly into 21, yielding three-foot-wide rings, each a walkable width.

Very neat and tidy, or so I thought. Ever since, and for the last many years, the journey of co-creating this labyrinth has been anything but neat and tidy. It is still unfinished and not yet the work of majesty I desire. But as I write these words I am reminded that neither the work of the

Divine nor the work of nature is ever really done. And my divine dance with nature involves being open, not trying to push or impose my will. Allowing the labyrinth to evolve in its own time is how nature works. And allowing divine majesty to bless each magnificent step of its unfolding is how I work.

And so I muddled on. That winter I studied seven-ring labyrinths and settled on a pattern from Minoan Crete, identified as perhaps the oldest known labyrinth pattern in the world. The next summer, I laid it out with construction flags because I couldn't yet imagine how I would ultimately craft this earthen but sacred work of art. And that winter, with the first significant snowfall, I walked it all the way in and all the way out and took a picture of the beautiful winding path I had left behind.

In the summer of 2009, I got inspired to develop the labyrinth as a botanical sanctuary garden for endangered wild medicinals: a healing place for people and plants. What joy to honor the spirit of the land by (re)introducing native wild medicinals and placing them under the care of surrounding guardian maple and butternut trees! After carefully sourced wild medicinals had been planted in, and the autumn chill quieted my garden busy-ness, I walked the labyrinth often, danced movement meditations in the center, and offered thanks.

Since then, my devotion to this dream has guided me to many awakenings: restoring the vitality of my soils; planting fruit and nut trees, shrubs, bushes, and vines; crafting flower essences and herbal medicinal oils, tinctures, and salves; and sitting with plants for many hours, conversing with their delightful spirits. After so many years suffering the ups and downs of eating addictions and marginal health, I have finally embraced a sincere commitment to nutrient-dense organic foods as the primary prescription for physical vibrancy and resilience. The divine dance in my backyard is an evolving dream in partnership with nature to enjoy a harmonious way of being human and caring for the Earth.

About ten years ago, on a cold November afternoon, while planting two Chinquapin chestnut trees in the backyard, I accidentally buried my wedding ring in the earth. I went berserk looking for it everywhere, hoping against hope that it hadn't really slipped off my cold and numb finger during that delicate process of gently guiding those tender roots into the nearly frozen ground. But I never found it. And I never could bring myself to disturb those delicate roots to dig it up, either.

Five years later, faced with a seemingly impossible choice of uprooting myself and moving far away to dutifully follow my husband to his new job, or staying in my beloved home on my beloved land … when that seemingly impossible choice finally became clear, I realized that at some point, maybe even on that cold November day at the very moment I buried my wedding ring, after a long courtship and gradual transfer of affection, I had in fact given up on the long and lonely marriage, and instead had married my land.

I enjoy a relationship with my land and with nature that flows harmoniously outside and inside of me in sacred communion. In this I have found the true happiness that somehow, even way back in the dark recesses of my therapist's office, I knew must be possible. Nature has shown me how to embody my ultimate purpose in this lifetime: to welcome her call into my heart and joyfully dance with the Divine.

"The idea that the 'material world' is not just a lump of resource, but reaches into every part of the realm of value, including the spiritual, that through our embodied nature we can commune with it, that there are responses and responsibilities that need to be respected, has largely been lost by the dominant culture."

—Iain McGilChrist,
The Master and his Emissary:
the Divided Brain and the Making of the Western World

About the Author

Katy Locke is a wanderer, visionary, and storyteller, living in wonder and awe most of the time, while cultivating a simple life of reverence, sacred inter-relationship, and magic. She takes great delight in the nooks and crannies of mountains and hills, oceans and streams, as well as the intricacies of the everyday. Katy has been writing about her unusual experiences and insights for many years, and is thrilled to be sharing tem in her first book.